Nicholas Clapp takes the reader on a ma
the rugged deserts and mountains of sou
the grace of a poet. His excursion into the mind and spirit of indigenous shamans leads us to better grasp the possible meaning of rock carvings and paintings left by those who came before us. Clapp goes to the very root of human experience and, augmented by stunning photographs, vividly shares his journey.

—*Richard L. Carrico,*
Professor of American Indian Studies,
San Diego State University.

A master storyteller, Nick Clapp artfully blends personal journey with published ethnographic impressions to transport the reader into the enigmatic nexus between California desert shamanism and rock art.

—*Steven M. Freers,*
rock art researcher and co-author of
Rock Art of the Grand Canyon *and* Fading Images

Introducing readers to beautifully photographed rock art, some fascinating stories and Indian legends, and plausible correlations between the art and the legends, *Old Magic* is a tour de force. What a delightful book!

—*Alan Grinnell,*
Research Associate, Fowler Museum,
and Associate Dean, Life Sciences, UCLA

Unveiling a hidden culture of the American southwest, *Old Magic* offers a fresh look at the way of the shaman in a compelling tour full of unexpected images. Bravo!

—*Martha Joukowsky,*
Brown University, Professor Emerita, Joukowsky Institute
of Archaeology and the Ancient World

Nicholas Clapp has conjured a persuasive story out of southern California's deserts, framed his tale with indigenous myths and traditions, and populated the landscape with the shamans that once negotiated with the spirits there. Gorgeously illustrated, *Old Magic* escorts us personally to rock art and relics that can still be encountered in remote canyons and on lost trails. These revelations of old California are no hocus-pocus but the real thing.

—Archeo-astronomer E.C. Krupp,
Director, Griffith Observatory,
and author of Skywatchers, Shamans, & Kings

As a friend of Carlos Castenada, I've long been fascinated by the world of the shaman. I was enthralled by *Old Magic*. I couldn't put it down; read it in a single sitting. It is a wonderful, insightful book, long overdue.

—William "Pete" Lee,
Director Emeritus, Los Angeles County Museum of Natural History,
and former Director of the Bowers Museum in Santa Ana

OLD MAGIC

OLD MAGIC

Lives of the Desert Shamans

Nicholas Clapp

Sunbelt Publications
San Diego

Old Magic: Lives of the Desert Shamans

Sunbelt Publications, Inc.
 First edition 2015, second edition 2017.

Edited by Anita Palmer
Cover and book design by Lydia D'moch
Project management by Deborah Young
Cartography by Kathleen Wise
Printed in the United States of America

 Please direct comments and inquiries to:

Sunbelt Publications, Inc.
P.O. Box 191126
San Diego, CA 92159-1126
(619) 258-4911, fax: (619) 258-4916
www.sunbeltpublications.com

20 19 18 17 5 4 3 2

Library of Congress Cataloging-in-Publication Data
Clapp, Nicholas.
Old magic : lives of the desert shamans / Nicholas Clapp.
pages cm
Includes bibliographical references and index.
ISBN 978-1-941384-05-3 (alk. paper)
1. Indians of North America–Mojave Desert–Religion.
2. Indians of North
America–Mojave Desert–Medicine 3. Shamanism–Mojave Desert.
4. Shamans–Mojave Desert. I. Title.
E78.S7C54 2014
299.7'11440979495–dc23 2014031074

All photographs are by the author unless noted or in public domain.

Cover: Shaman Bill Kawitch of the Western Shoshone dwelt on the edge of *tiwiingarivipi*, the "sacred land, mythic country" of the desert tribes of the Far West. The accompanying rock art is from that land, and may well be a portrait of a shaman in a dream state accompanied by an animal spirit helper. It has been attributed to shaman Bob Rabbit of the Shoshone/Kawii.

Page ii: **Shaman Old Bob of the Mono Paiute.**

For Bonnie,
who knew where to look.

A shaman's cave. Western Sonoran Desert.

Contents

Author's Note

No question: Desert shamans were pieces of work—complex, charismatic, scary even.

Their everyday life was little different than that of others of their clan, a matter of survival in a harsh, unforgiving land. But then, called to doctor an ailment, they would conjure dreamscape visions—miasmic visions that could psychically fly them to the land of the dead, a journey that could prove perilous and possibly fatal.

As might be expected, it has been a challenge to explore and make sense of lives such as these, and accordingly, the author assumes full responsibility for any missteps or misinterpretations.

The role of rock art is a case in point, with anthropological caution long a byword. Yet now there are theories and sufficient collateral evidence to venture fresh, if tentative, interpretations. There is no question that rock art panels express *something*. The question is *what.* And to me, *not* wondering what they depict is akin to dismissing Egyptian tomb paintings with a shrug, or eye-rolling a Picasso. So it is that on occasion I have ventured to relate rock art—not all, but some of it—to a shaman's arcane calling.

(To protect rock art sites, specific locations are given only if they are identified—and signed—by national parks, state parks, or other government agencies.)

Prologue

Though it was his day off, Deputy Sheriff Bryan Smalley nevertheless slipped his revolver into its scuffed, duty-worn holster. "Never know what you're going to find out there," he muttered, then brightened with, "Bonnie and Nick, what you'll see today will knock you out!" He whistled. Three dogs leapt into the battered bed of his Ford pickup. He eyed and kicked the tires. "Needs sealant when we get back. Slows the leaks."

Westward out of Goldfield, with a plume of desert dust in our wake, we crossed Nevada's sparsely-populated Esmeralda County. This was Bryan's beat, Bryan's world. Down by Clayton dry lake, he mused, he'd pried a drunk from a wreck; off in the Montezuma hills a lost and befuddled, yet arrogant individual had, via cell phone, demanded immediate rescue. "Only problem he had absolutely no idea where he was. I asked him to describe what exactly he saw around him. Figured it out. Went and got him. Was he grateful, the jerk? No."

Bryan's feeling for his Nevada landscape stretched back in time. Not long ago, he'd happened on a cluster of barely-recognizable graves, the possible site of a wagon train massacre. And ahead now, in the Silver Peak Mountains, he'd discovered site-after-site of Indian petroglyphs.

The road wound up into the mountains, dwindled to barely passable ruts, and gave out. On foot, dogs bounding and barking, Bryan made for and, with amazing alacrity, climbed a rocky bluff. Bonnie and I followed. "Right ahead," he pointed out, "Neat, huh?" Two does, peacefully grazing, were etched in the flat face of a boulder (on previous page).- Bryan scampered on. "And down here, how about this?" A hunter had set three dogs on a doomed stag.

"And look down there. They hung out down there, worked their magic. Shamans."

At the foot of the bluff, semi-circles of rocks echoed mysterious rings Bonnie and I had investigated in southern California's Anza-Borrego Desert State Park, close by our home.

"Shamans?" Bonnie asked, "They were here?"

"For sure," answered Bryan, "Come out here on a moonlit night. You'll feel it. You bet."

With scenes and symbols the breadth of the its steeply pitched face, the bluff was a veritable magic mountain of petroglyphs. There was more to be seen. All that day, we clambered up and down a dozen similar sites, etched with as many as a thousand petroglyphs. A host of desert animals . . . strange, abstract symbols . . . elongated, other-worldly human figures. What did they represent? What was their point, their purpose? An extraordinary panel portrayed dancers, or at least what I thought were dancers, their postures similar to those of Yaqui deer dancers I'd seen down by the Mexican border. Bryan, on the other hand, thought this to be a record of a battle. Or we both could be right: dancers could be re-enacting a battle.

"The circle over that dancer's head," Bonnie said, "It's like a halo."

I wondered, could he be a shaman? Shamans, I'd read, had an affinity for circles and spirals.

It was hot, and we were now miles from the Ford. Bryan fanned himself with his dusty black hat. "Magic," he said, "old magic." This became a refrain as we retraced our steps. He'd look up, address the stark mountains; he'd look down, shake his head and murmur, "old magic . . ."

The sun was setting as, back in the pickup, we detoured to a last site. Bryan slowed, cranked down his window, peered into a shadowy cave. "It's shallow, not much to see, in fact nothing to see. But it was home to Esmeralda County's last shaman. A rickety old guy, died in the 1950s." He popped the clutch; we headed back to Goldfield.

"Old magic . . ."

To me, and to Bonnie as well, the words conjured the workings of medieval wizards and witches, steeped in pentacles and spells harkening to an even older magic, the magic of the mysterious East. Staffs turned to snakes in Pharaoh's court.

But what Bryan had in mind was a wilder magic, a magic of wanderers though shadowy jungles and forests—and windswept, icy wastes. In 1698 the word and concept of "shaman" was reported as a component of the life of Turkish-Tungusic folk of eastern Siberia. And long before that, Siberian shamans had, via a Bering Strait land bridge, made their way from the Old World to the New, where they were both feared and revered by tribes from Alaska to Tierra del Fuego. They could cure the sick, charm game, fly through the air, journey to the land of the dead and return. Or if of a malign bent, they could curse and kill one's enemies. So it was said and believed.

For millennia, shamans held sway in the New World, until the day came that for all their real or vaunted power, they were helpless in countering the invasion—and proselytization—of Spanish, then Anglo, settlers.

With an exception, a hold-out.

In the far desert West, beyond the reach of meddlers and missionaries, shamanism remained a force well into the late 1800s, even into the early 1900s. And how shamanism was practiced—what it was all about—would have become a distant, confused memory had it not been for the vision and drive of one Alfred L. Kroeber.

Berkeley's Alfred L. Kroeber

A Berkeley professor, Kroeber was possessed by a desperate need to record, if not preserve, native American traditions. From 1901 on, he doggedly sought out anyone who was willing to spend time in the field, anyone who could collect and sort data, and write it up. Had Deputy Smalley been around, he'd have been an ideal recruit. Kroeber's army was a dedicated, often rag-tag, sometimes eccentric lot—of college students, amateur historians, curious school teachers, Indian agents, daft desert loners.

Their enterprise would be "salvage ethnology."

Kroeber's researchers found native Americans to be willing subjects. There would always be a measure of their world—rightly so—kept secret. Yet they realized that, if it wasn't shared, the essence of their spiritual heritage might be forever lost.

Particular attention was paid to the beliefs—and shamanism—of the Cahuilla of the western Sonoran Desert. At home in a hostile environment, the Cahuilla appeared the least beholden to outside influences. And hearteningly, in the wake of the Berkeley studies, the Cahuilla themselves would document their culture. In 1980, Ruby Modesto, a surviving Cahuilla shaman, collaborated on an account aptly titled *Not for Innocent Ears*. And before that, in 1939, Chief Francisco Patencio of the tribe's Palm Springs branch, penned a remembrance of what he learned from his mother, "very old and blind. When she talked everyone listened. These old people talked like a book. There are not any more left now. Now the old people are like all old people."

And if one heeds the desert's rocks, there is now even more to draw on.

For the longest time, Indian petroglyphs and pictographs were dismissed as "seemingly aimless chipping" and "a diversion of an idle people."[1] Yet as early as Garrick Malery's 1893 *Picture-Writing of the*

1 Petroglyhs are pecked on blackened, desert-varnished rock; pictographs are painted with naturally occurring pigments mixed with a binder, often blood. Both are rock art. The quote is from W.L. Chalfant, *The Story of Inyo*, p. 25 and 27.

American Indians, doughty researchers took issue with this, even as they were stumped as to the rock art's intent and meaning. They believed some of it to mark borders, record battles, bring luck in the hunt. But what of its jumbles of strangely abstract patterns—and bizarre, unearthly figures?

To the rescue came the ground-breaking work of researchers spearheaded by Ken Hedges of the San Diego Museum of Man and David Whitley of the University of California, Los Angeles. From the 1970s on, they linked rock art of the far desert West to lives and practices of shamans, and offered insights—often startling—into their hidden world.[2] Here was a new and unexpected window on Deputy Bryan's "old magic."

—*Nicholas Clapp*
Borrego Springs, California

2 It is a far-reaching world. Garrick Malery's 1893 survey reported a dozen rock art locales in the deserts of eastern California and western Nevada. Now, as many as 35,000 sites have been recorded.

Shaman self-portraits. Western Sonoran Desert.

Of Tribes and Territories

The boundaries on this map (opposite) are arbitrary—as they were to the tribes roaming its desert realm. With survival ever an issue, they sought game where they could and shared springs and wells. To pioneering writer Mary Austin, this was "a country of lost borders."

This shifting, wandering world had, to a degree, a social and cultural unity—of shared myths and survival arts, reinforced by trade and intermarriage. This was a contrast to the life of the settled, self-contained Pueblo tribes off to the east. And there was a further distinction. The Navajo, the Hopi, the Zuni—all had a highly structured belief system expressed in kiva rituals honoring gods of the earth and sky and a host of katsina (or kachina) spirits.

This wasn't a fit for tribes of the open desert and their small bands living as best they could, wherever they could. What did work was a reliance on individuals who had been favored with spiritual power, magical power.

Shamans.

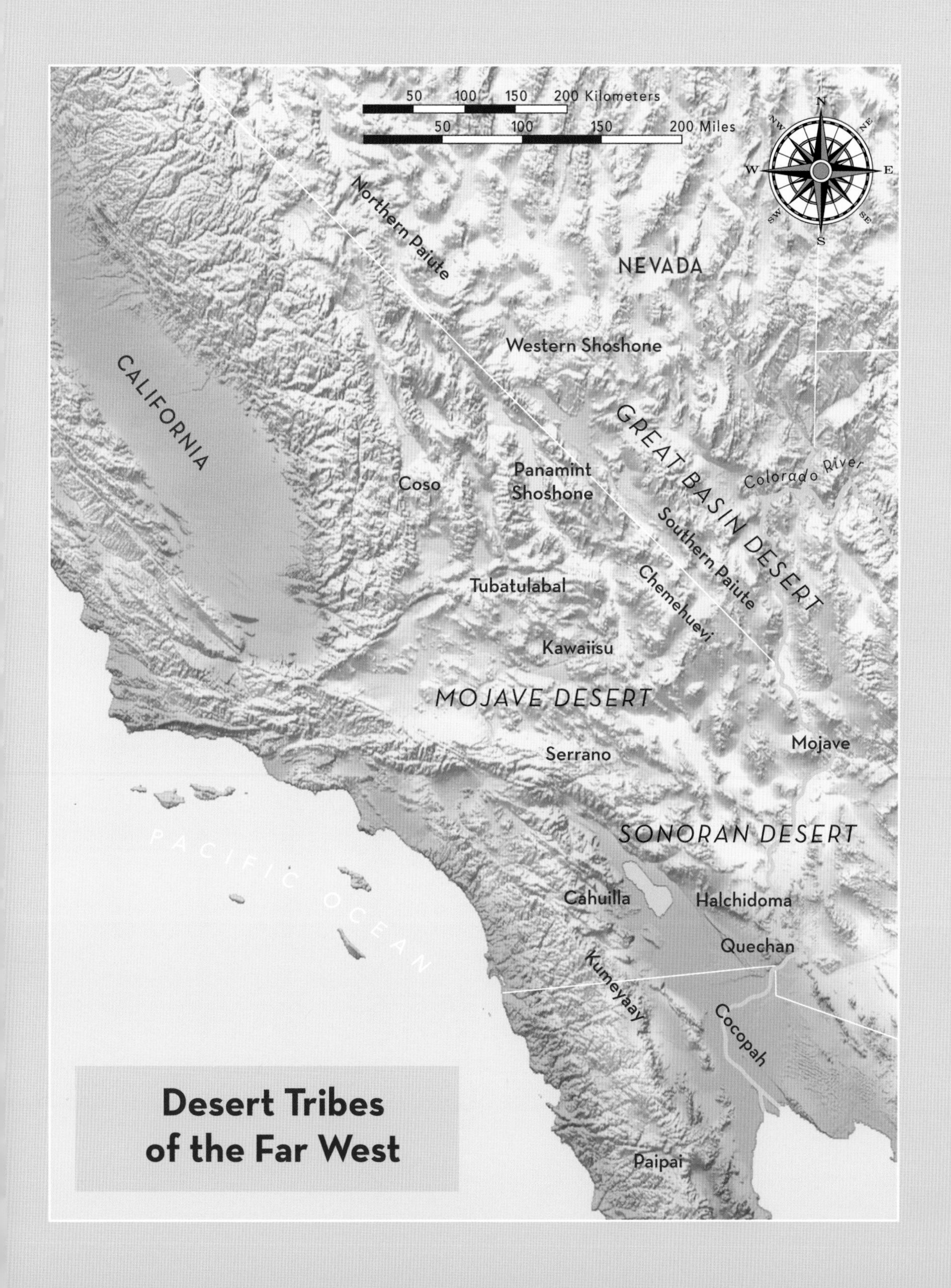

Desert Tribes of the Far West

Part One

The Way of the Shaman

Dawn

GATHERED IN THE NIGHT, a mist shrouds the lower Colorado River. Slowly, from off to the east, a hazy glow gives form to the still waters of riverside meanders and marshes, dense with stands of mesquite, tule, and cattail.

Then: a muffled flapping and a piercing cry.

Gliding low to the water, a bald eagle spies a Colorado River toad. Alarmed, the plump creature dives to the safety of marsh-bottom muck. No matter. Dawn is the time of the hunt, and a minute or so later, the eagle spies less fortunate prey and, talons outstretched, homes in on a fish, snake, or a riverbank rabbit frozen with fear.

The sun crests the horizon; the morning mist dissolves.

The eagle continues its hunt, spiraling upward, higher and yet higher, to soar over the Mojave Desert's rugged, soon burning expanse. And as an eagle is an icon of majesty and power, far below there is another icon—a graven image of a mighty giant.

A few miles west of the Colorado River:
a Quechan pilgrimage site. Note the giant
figure of Kumastamxo, one of six in the area.

Born of an ancient dawn, his name was Kumastamxo.

Among the Quechan people of the lower Colorado River, his story was told around flickering campfires and in tribal lodges. In the past; even now.

This Kumastamxo created the sun and stars, and offered seeds to the progenitors of the tribes of the Quechan, the Kumeyaay, and the

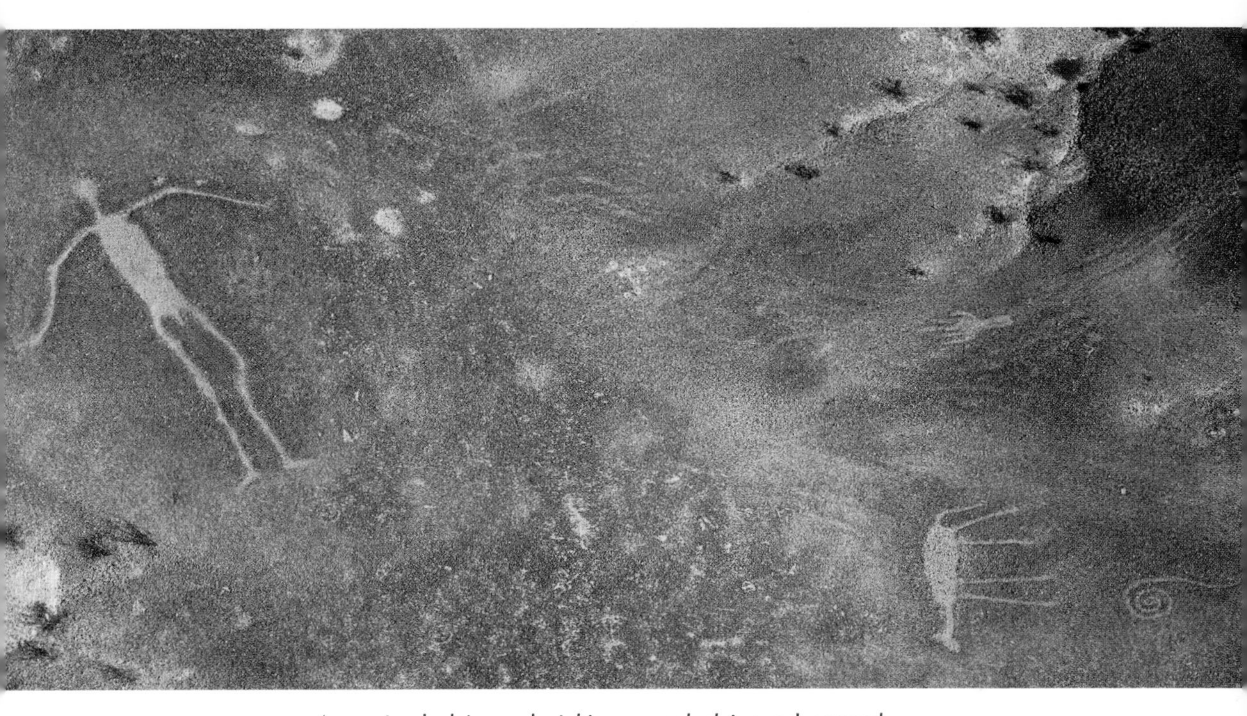

As a petroglyph is a rock etching, a geoglyph is a rock-scraped, often enormous earth etching. If upright, this image of Kumastamxo would rise to the height of a ten story building.

Maricopa. And close by he was attended by a first shaman—a mountain lion, for back then, animals could be shamans. If you look closely, there's a swirl of water by the cat's front feet—the Colorado River. Upon Kumastamxo striking the ground with his spear, its waters poured forth. With his spear, he marked its winding course.

Avikwa'ame, Spirit Mountain, also called Dead Mountain. (Now known as Newberry Peak, eastern Mojave Desert.)

He next gathered men—shamans he had created—and together they boarded a raft and drifted downriver with the current. They encountered a great serpent, and Kumastamxo demonstrated his power by slaying Sky-rattlesnake.

He then led his shamans to the heights of Avikwa'ame, Spirit Mountain, where in a Dark House built by animals, he instructed them in sacred and magical and doctoring ways. They became powerful men, these primordial shamans. They could order the earth to groan and quake; they left footprints in solid rock.

Happy with what he had passed on, Kumastamxo dismissed his shamans, and sank into the earth, to be reborn as an eagle.

The eagle flew up to the mountain's Dark House, to forever dwell in its shadows.

The site of the eagle's death and ghostly transfiguration—Avikwa'ame—was noted in the year 1861 by the first American party to chart the lower Colorado River:

> It is the highest peak in sight and is regarded with reverence by the Indians, who believe it to be the abode of their departed spirits. Ireteba [a translator] informed me that any one dare to visit it, he would be struck dead.
>
> Indians are seated at the verge of the camp, earnestly observing the Dead Mountain. Its hoary crest is draped in a light floating haze, and misty wreaths are winding like phantoms among its peaks and dim recesses. The wondering watchers see the spirits hovering above their legendary abode, and gaze reverently at the shadowy forms that circle around its haunted summit.[3]

Here was an awe shared by the Army's Lt. Joseph Christmas Ives and his topographic crew. And here, there was a marked divergence from their Judeo-Christian heritage and beliefs, in which the Almighty remained unquestionably *almighty*. A God of gods, supremely powerful. To the contrary, the creator Kumastamxo was to cede his power—his control of man and nature—upon sinking into the earth.

A question, then, was: Who or what was to inherit that power? Step into that cosmic vacuum?

An answer, it would appear, was: *shamans*. They are key to the Quechan creation account.

And, to most all of the desert tribes, varying words for *shaman* signified "a man of power."

Intrigued by this, my wife, Bonnie, and I sought further, related creation accounts. Of the Chemehuevi, the Mohave, the Shoshone, and Paiute. And where we live, the Kumeyaay and Desert Cahuilla. The core story was the same, one tribe to the next.

At the same time, we were on the lookout for rock art sites that might (or might not) portray aspects of creation. Bonnie, I discovered, had a

3 Lt. Joseph C. Ives, *Report upon the Colorado River of the West*, p. 75 and 80.

preternatural, almost alarming instinct as to just where we should clamber.

"Up under that boulder," she'd point up a slope.

"You think so?"

"Has to be."

And she'd be right—as with petroglyphs and pictographs of *the three puzzling suns*. She would find them, over and over again, in nooks and crannies of distant corners of the desert.[4] The very best site proved to be close to home: a cave in California's Anza-Borrego Desert State Park.

4 Though the images could be of stars or even flowers, we settled on suns as defined in Bernard M. Jones, Jr., "Shamanic Symbols: Visual Metaphors in Rock Art Images," as well as in Alex Paterson, *Rock Art Symbols of the Greater Southwest.*

Our first thought was that the cave's three suns once served as solstice markers, only to have this notion fade with the realization that throughout the day they were shaded, and well beyond the reach of the sun. We were stumped. But then, as the site was in Kumeyaay territory, we searched their lore and legends for a significant mention of suns, and found one—just one—in the story of how their creator-god, Chiapa-Komat—was displeased with a world shrouded in darkness. Chiapa-Komat flung a ball of yellow mud into the sky—it became the moon. Its light, though, was disappointingly pale, cause for Chiapa-Komat to hurl a ball of red mud skyward—which became the sun.

It dawned upon us that these three enigmatic suns could well be markers—waypoints—in the Kumeyaay's creation story. Regrettably, what further survives of that story is brief, fragmentary, and a bit muddled. But this is not the case with the account treasured—to this day—by their neighbors, the Desert Cahuilla.

Here then—in the eyes of the Cahuilla—is how the sun, banishing darkness, came to radiate life and power. (With Kumeyaay rock art suns serving as waypoints.)

The Time of the Black Sun (Of Darkness, Then Light)

There was no earth or sky, no one, nothing but darkness. But then the darkness stirred. It was alive! And it rumbled with eerie sounds, as if risen from the throats of faraway singers. From time to time, lightning, or something like lightning, would flash, and glisten on the strands of what appeared to be a spider web, and in it, two very large eggs. They hatched, and two boys emerged, first Mukat and then his twin Tamaioit. In darkness, they sought someone to talk to and play with, which led them each in his way to create people.

To bring light to a pitch-black world, Mukat created Lizard. Lizard tried to swallow darkness, but failed. So together, the two brothers Mukat and Tamaioit created Moon, a woman bright and beautiful and white.

Mukat could now see Tamaioit's people. Mukat didn't like them, not at all. They had faces on both the front and backs of their heads. Way too many toes pointed both ahead and behind them. And not only their toes, but their fingers were webbed, like a duck's.

The first brothers quarreled, as brothers have quarreled ever since.

Tamaiot was furious. If what he'd fashioned wasn't appreciated, he threatened to abandon his brother.

And he did just that.

Wildly singing, Tamaiot sank into the earth, taking the people he'd made with him.

An awful time ensued. The sky blackened, and fire flew. Earthquakes rocked a once smooth and serene earth. Mountains jutted skyward.

Then everything settled down and all was quiet. The sun shone, as it does now. Mukat, now unchallenged in his powers, put the finishing touches on creation. A world of peace and harmony was at hand.

The Time of the Yellow-Red Sun (And of a Creator-God's Death)

It was then, in the eyes of his people, that Mukat erred. He ordered Rattlesnake to bite an innocent little man, beloved by all. He then gave his people bows and arrows, and shrugged as they killed one another, this after promising that no harm would befall them. Finally, a night came when Mukat became enthralled with the radiant beauty of Moon, his daughter. A terrible thing, too terrible to mention, happened, and deeply saddened, Moon, that very night, left Mukat and her people. So no one would follow her, she persuaded beetles and ants to crawl over her tracks.

Everyone felt badly, very badly. They tried and failed to find Moon. Children cried and cried, until the next night they were surprised to see Moon's face rippling in a spring. They looked up: above the horizon, she smiled down on them, and ever since has watched over little children.

Their faith in Mukat shattered, his people decided to kill him.

From a branch a bird, a flicker, sang, "Let's witch him." But who would do this? "Not me, not me!" everyone exclaimed. Then someone suggested: "Let Frog do it," and all took up the cry. So it was that when Mukat went by night to relieve himself, Frog devoured his droppings.

Right away, Mukat knew something was wrong, for he felt very ill and weak, as though his soul had left his body. He implored his shamans to help him. They pretended to, but didn't really try, for they wanted him to die. Mukat's sole friend now was Coyote. But who could trust Coyote?

Frog worked his magic. Mukat shook uncontrollably. He stiffened and died.

As he was cremated, his people, every one of them, cried. Mukat's heart was the last of him to burn, which prompted Coyote to burst through the crowd, seize it with his teeth, and run off into the mountains. The blood strains are there, still to be seen.

So concludes the Cahuilla' creation story.

And at this point, consider this: Weep as they might, the Cahuilla had killed their creator, and they were not alone. One way or another, the tale's dark conclusion—of a diminished or disposable creator-god—was shared by tribes throughout the far western desert.

There would, however, remain a deep respect for what Mukat had created, an abiding reverence for "everywhere the spirits" of the earth and sky, with a special awe for the life-giving, fiery power of the sun. Even so, in myth—and indeed, in everyday tribal life—there was now a void.

Mukat, once powerful beyond measure, was no more. Yet the power he possessed remained—in rocks, clouds, the sun, in all the forces of nature. In a host of power animals ranging from a dragonfly to a bighorn sheep.

It was a power ripe to be acquired.

By shamans.

In rituals and magical dreams, shamans could now assume the role of the creator-god they had willfully let die. This was to initiate an era that would last a thousand generations, and endure to the time of the white man.

The Time of the Third Sun (Of a Double-Ringed Shaman's Sun)

There was untold power in this final sun, and the nature of that power is reflected and revealed in a major geoglyph twenty miles east of the cave sheltering the three suns. Here, a 650 foot, snake-like path winds across the desert to two concentric circles. In 1989, Chief Tom Lucas, a last survivor of the local Kwaaymii clan, interpreted the site.[5] The land outside the outer circle, the old chief explained, represented the power all things possess, the power that enables earthly existence.

The power within the outer circle was stronger, and was accessible to humans through prayer or spiritual quests.

None but a shaman could set foot in the power-laden inner circle. At its center, a hub of quartz cobbles evoked the essence of a world

5 Recorded in the late Jay von Werlhof's "E = MC2: Implications of Power in Yuha Desert Geoglyphs," pp. 30–1.

forfeit to shamans upon the mythic demise of their creator-god. They and they alone could enter, explore, and manipulate the inner circle's awesome forces.

For good, or as we shall see, for evil.

For power is amoral.

The Eagle Dance

Over years and centuries, shamans assured the Cahuilla that it was right and proper for their forbears to have slain Mukat. But, nod in agreement as they might, the Cahuilla forever lamented the act. And this state of mind—conflicted yet determined—was echoed in an annual ceremonial killing of *Ahswit*, an eagle.

When Berkeley-dispatched anthropologist William Strong spent time among the Cahuilla in the early 1900s, he documented living memories of the rite. The details he set down were sufficiently vivid to suggest that it may still have been practiced in remote villages.

In mountain crags, the Cahuilla had long sought the nests of eagles, and guarded them as eggs were laid and fledglings hatched. The young were then captured and carefully tended until they had acquired their full plumage.

On an appointed night, the people danced, a slow circular dance around a fire—and by the fire, a shaman cradled an eagle wrapped in a ceremonial mat.

Sometime before dawn, the eagle would "scream and die," most likely killed (Strong thought) by the compression of its lungs.

With great care, the body was laid by the fire. The dancing stopped. Wracked with sorrow, the dancers wept and wailed as long ago their forebears had lamented the death of Mukat.

The meaning of this is at once clear and elusive. An ancient event had been re-enacted. But why? What was at stake? What was to be gained? Berkeley researcher Lowell John Bean, for one, believed the rite—of sacrifice and death—offered promise and assurance. In his words, "The eagle is said to live forever, and yet from the 'beginning' allowed himself to be 'killed' so the people were assured of life after death."[6]

If that was the case, what is interesting is that this assurance would naturally have been offered by a shaman, not a god, or even a priest speaking on behalf of a god. Shamans were key figures in the eagle rite.

Indeed, occasions were reported when several shamans would gather and each in turn, without laying a hand on the eagle, would attempt to kill it with their personal power. A shaman with little power would momentarily agitate the eagle, but that was all. A second shaman might repeatedly strike his own head, and the eagle would scream and droop its head, but not die. Yet another shaman would step into the fire, stand there, and point at the eagle with magical sticks; the bird would visibly droop, but then recover.

6 Lowell John Bean, *Mukat's People*, p. 139.

Drooping bird and a mask of death. Southern Mojave Desert.

Shamans might dance, sing, and work their magic the night through to kill an eagle, as in myth their forebears had precipitated the death of another icon, their creator Mukat. If—improbably—the bird survived, it was set free. Their power challenged, their efficacy doubted, the assembled shamans would hasten off to their scattered huts.

Theirs was not an easy life. Brokering power, consorting with the supernatural, even psychically journeying to the land of the dead, their way was fraught with peril—and madness.

Old magic was to have its price.

Signs

THOUGH STARK, often brutally so, the land's mountains, badlands, and plains provided sustenance to a stalwart tribe. As myth has it, the Cahuilla, soon after creation, had embarked on an arduous and far-ranging journey in search of a new homeland. Only to have the quest end where it began: back in the desert.

There being no place they'd rather live. It was a land with a soul. It was alive with spirits. Spirits of animals. At their grandparents' and parents' knees, little children learned their names, their good qualities and bad. Birds, deer, and bighorn sheep were benign and friendly. But watch out for coyote; he was sly and clever, often too clever for his own good. Rattlesnakes and wild cats—they evoked a mix of awe, fright, and respect.

Cahuilla youngsters dreamed of animals, possibly even more than they dreamed of people. And they came to believe that all nature was a realm of spirits. Spirits dwelt in plants, and in the sun, moon, and clouds—even rocks. There was magic in rocks. And stars.

Beyond southern California's coastal range: the territory of the Desert Cahuilla.

A child's world was enchanted—and harsh. Extended families drifted from camp to camp, surviving in the winter months on mesquite and agave in the open desert, and in the summer, acorns harvested up winding canyons. Rarely was there game; even rarer, plentiful game.

In the Cahuilla's unsettled life, there was a critical need—for *puls*, their word for shamans. Puls to cure ills; puls to foresee the future; puls to guide their uncertain fortunes.

So it was that tribal elders had an eye out for children with an affinity for the otherworldly, the spiritual—a child touched by unseen forces, a child who by night gazed into the darkness beyond the cooking fire. Often, these were six or seven year olds who cried a lot or were given to sick spells, and a doctoring pul would sense that one day, the child might become a "man of power." Or woman of power.

Or a child might talk in his or her sleep, and try to sing. Though the song might be unintelligible, it was a sign.

Frequently, a calling to be a shaman came in a dream conjured by the spirit of a desert animal. A child would often keep this to himself, and try to forget it. He'd not confide the dream, not even to his parents. Then, unsolicited, there'd be more dreams. A child would worry, perceiving a

Anza-Borrego Desert State Park, once Cahuilla territory.
(Beyond the two distant buttes lay the territory of their neighbors, the Kumeyaay.)

pul's life to be lonely, arduous, even dangerous. The spirits would persist in tempting him, and testing his resolve and power. The spirits weren't always nice. They just might visit death, it was whispered, on a child who rejected their call.

A youngster could refuse the calling, as did Francisco Patencio, who as an adult would become chief of the Cahuilla dwelling at Palm Springs. He related, "I used to get messages to be a medicine man when I was a small boy. But I never told, and I never used it [the power]."

The opposite was the case with Ruby Modesto, possibly the last of the Cahuilla puls. "I was a born dreamer," she recounted,

> My mother used to take me to the Moravian Church here on the Reservation. I always fell asleep and my soul would fly right out of the building through a little hole in the ceiling. I was a

> Christian for a long time. . . . But now I know that you cannot be a Christian and a pul too. You have to choose between them, because Christians teach that a pul gets power from the devil, and I don't believe that. . . .[7]

Ruby's great uncle Charlie, a pul, encouraged her to dream on.

At the age of ten, Ruby's dream life intensified, beckoning her to strange and enchanted worlds—or as she called them, "levels." The first level was an ordinary dream. But then, *within that dream . . .*

> You consciously tell yourself to lay down and go to sleep. Then you dream a second dream. This is the second level and the prerequisite for real Dreaming. Uncle Charlie called this process "setting up dreams." You can tell yourself ahead of time where you want to go, or what you want to see, or what you want to learn.
>
> On the third level you learn and see unusual things, not of this world. The hills and terrain are different. On both the second and third dream levels you can talk to people and ask questions about what you want to know. During dreaming the soul goes out of the body, so you have to be careful.
>
> When I dreamed to the thirteenth level, that first time, I was young and didn't know how to get back. Usually I only dream to the second or third levels. But that time I kept having different dreams and falling asleep and going to another dream level. That was where I met my helper, *Ahswit*, the eagle. But I was in sort of a coma, asleep for several days. My father tried to bring me back, but couldn't. He had to call my Uncle Charlie who finally managed to bring my spirit back. That was one of his specialties,

7 This and the following quote from Ruby Modesto and Guy Mount, *Not for Innocent Ears*, p. 27 and 26–7.

Ruby Modesto, a life-long Cahuilla pul.

healing soul loss. When I woke up they made me promise not to Dream like that again, not until I knew how to get back by myself. The way you return is to tell yourself beforehand that you are going to come back, and later in the dream you have to remember this. Once, I was dreaming on the third level and wondering how I was going to return. Suddenly a giant bird appeared, like a pelican: it came along and I grabbed its neck. We flew way up in the sky. I saw the earth burning below and I sort of came out of it into the second level dream. It's really hard to come out of those higher levels.

On her night sky journeys, Ruby encountered a multitude of creatures: deer, lizard, even a gray fly who proclaimed, "I'm going to play a song. I'm a virtuoso!" Informed of this the next morning, Ruby's mother believed her daughter was losing her mind (and in a way, she was). Ruby insisted, "I heard that fly talk just as plain as people." Accordingly, Ruby's parents gave their strange child "my Indian name, Nesha, which means 'woman of mystery'." Charlie, Nesha's great uncle, saw it coming. "Uncle Charlie always said that a real pul is born, destined to be one in the womb."

With other youngsters, the signs were ambiguous, not altogether clear. But then, as both girls and boys came of age, the time came for them to be instructed in tribal lore and secrets, and be offered a glimpse of a world beyond anything they could have imagined.

They would become *puplem—the initiated.*[8]

8 For the Cahuilla, initiation and shamanism were linguistically linked. The word pul (shaman) is derivative of puplem (the initiated).

Strange clouds over a spirit-haunted landscape.

A Cahuilla maiden of the 1890s.
Right: A diamondback, common to the desert.

Coming of Age

SHIMMERING WITH HEAT WAVES, blindingly bright, the desert's landscape evoked an elemental spiritual awe. The Cahuilla, the Kumeyaay, and the Quechan expressed this awe in song cycles—Lightning songs, Bird Songs—recounting shared concepts of creation and wandering; of how in life to walk a straight, not crooked path; and what becomes of a man or woman's soul upon their death.

Initiation: Girls

As a next generation came of age, there was much to be taught, much to be passed on.

For girls, a first menstruation would be cause for an initiatory ordeal—a "roasting." A girl's family and her people would assemble, and an elder—often a shaman—would three times blow to the skies, then place a ball of tobacco in the girl's mouth and order her to swallow it. Bear in mind that this wasn't the white man's tobacco; it was wild, acrid, native tobacco. Yet if a girl vomited, her virtue was in question. It was admitted, "This was a hard test."[9]

At best wobbly—as the tobacco took a narcotic hold on her senses—the girl was now escorted to a several-foot deep "vision pit." It had been filled with scalding hot stones that, on her approach, were snatched away and replaced with a lining of brush, sedge, and grass. The girl was laid out on her back, and to ward off flies, a loosely woven basket was slipped over her head. Two warm, flat stones were placed on her abdomen, so that as a woman she would enjoy good health, and not be wrinkled or go gray.

For three days she lay as still as possible, only rising from the pit when, from time to time, it was reheated. Some clans as well offered her a daily respite in a warmed hut. By night old men and women circled the pit, dancing and singing a song that Moon had taught the people before Moon was assaulted by her creator-father, and fled to the sky. The song instructed girls how to look after themselves, particular during their menstrual periods, periods timed to Moon's waxing and waning. It was a song of innocence lost.

Her vision occluded, the girl would slip in out of consciousness. Heightened by the tobacco she had ingested, it was a trance-time, a time for visions of an animal—as tiny as an ant or as big as a bear—that might become her spirit guardian.

Raised from the pit, the woman—no longer a girl—had her face painted with red, zig-zag diamond designs, a rattlesnake motif. Joined by friends and other initiates, a spirited footrace ensued, with a long life to the winner. The goal was a special boulder, painted with the same design as on the woman's face.

Initiates would in time bear children, and witness their daughters come of age. Some would, monthly, return to their vision pits and dream,

9 Quoted in Alfred L. Kroeber, *Handbook of the Indians of California*, p. 674.

A possible initiation boulder. Blair Valley, western Sonoran Desert.
Below: Detail of red over an older yellow design.

for in the words of Ruby Modesto, "Dreams were the source of all wisdom." She recalled that men as well had their vision pits, further from a village or camp, way up in the mountains.

A few, very few women—either after their "roasting" or in place of it, would join the initiation of boys in their clan. For the Cahuilla, this was an annual rite overseen by puls. Puls had a minimal role in a girl's initiation; they dominated a boy's.

A Desert Cahuilla ceremonial enclosure.

Initiation: Boys

With branches and mud, a pul would construct a temporary dwelling in a remote locale, and for an intense week, five to ten boys (and every so often a young woman) would be schooled in Cahuilla ways. They were to respect their elders and be kind to strangers. Anger was bad; stealing was worse. If he walked a straight path, a man would grow old in good health, and upon his death be praised and have his spirit live on in the sky. But if a man's path was crooked, misfortune would beset him. And at this point the lecture would often lapse into a harangue.

Disobedient? Rattlesnake and spider will vie to bite you. You will swell up, vomit blood, go lame, cough your lungs out. Heedless? Expect your eyes to granulate, your children to sicken. Lie or deceive? All manner of animals will rise up as death-dealing avengers. Even if just indolent, "See this! Raven will shoot you with bow and arrow!"[10]

The Cahuilla's *kikisulem*. In Spanish: *toloache*. In English: *jimsonweed, Devil's weed, thorn apple, loco weed, moonflower, sacred datura* or *deadly datura*. (Botanically, *datura wrightii*.)

In the intense, close quarters of the pul-built house, initiates-to-be were called upon to memorize a multitude of songs held sacred, and were "smoked upon" by shamans arriving from neighboring clans. And the boys witnessed magic, the likes of a feather headdress thrust into flames and not consumed, or a pul's tongue cut out and restored.

Then and even now there was the question: how real was a pul's magic? It was never to be fully answered, though a case has been made that shamans—"gifted with a low cunning"—were known to be tricksters. That was apparently fine by the Cahuilla and like tribes. The gasp . . . the effect . . . the drama was what counted.

About the same time initiates-to-be were confined, a knowledgeable pul scoured desert ridges and valleys in search of "grass that could talk": *kikisulem*—a delicately-ribbed, trumpet-like flower.

The plant was revered as a magical, living spirit. The pul would address it as "Old Woman," and apologize for disturbing it. With ritual care and respect, he would dig its east-pointing root from the earth and set about "cooking it"—drying the root, a root intense with power.

10 *Ibid*, p. 684.

Toloache mortar.

At the end of a week's confinement, the initiates-to-be emerged from their schooling, and were taken to a brush enclosure where, on the coming of the night, a fire was lit and a crowd gathered.

Earlier the same day, a ceremonial stone mortar would have been dug from its hiding place, to be cleaned and repainted. In common, the desert's tribes recognized it as a "toloache mortar," *toloache* being the Spanish name for kikisulem. Chanting softly, a pul ground the kikisulem's root, then dissolved its powder in water and let the concoction stand.

Parents worried, as well they should. Kikisulem would clarify the blood and mind. It could also kill.

One by one, the boys now knelt before the mortar, to take one or more sips. A watchful pul would jerk a boy back when, for his age and size, he'd had enough.

The boys would then rise up, and dance. Faster and faster yet, spiraling as a whirlwind. Parents and old people joined in. (Sometimes, it was reported, a man or woman would trip and fall in the fire, but not be burned.)

The drug was potent and fast acting.

The initiates staggered, and one-by-one, crumpled to the ground. They foamed at the mouth. For a time they might murmur or even shriek as animals. This was a good sign; an animal spirit helper was nigh.

The boys would sink into a stupor—a stupor, it was believed, in which they would glimpse what the future had in store for them.

And they'd become men.

Attendant puls would carry them off to a secluded spot—and every few years, they carried a boy to his grave.

Dancing on, parents and old people circled the fire three times, and sat down. At a signal from a pul, three hoarse grunting sounds rose from their throats. They then tilted back their heads and repeatedly raised their arms to the stars, each time noisily expelling their breath. The puls among them jumped up and with their bare feet, stamped out the fire.

The comatose boys were watched the night through, and when in the morning they stirred, they were given copious amounts of warm water to dilute the kikisulem's hallucinatory effect. They had dreamed as they'd never dreamt before. Near all had encountered an animal that had pledged to become their life-long spirit helper. The animal, they reported, assured them of the role they would play—as men—in the life of their clan. This confirmed, they'd never again partake kikisulem.

For one, possibly two men, there had been more to the experience. Their initiatory dream would have been vivid verging on ecstatic. They'd raptly listened as their spirit helper taught them things. Songs often, songs that could cure, assure luck in the hunt, or bring rain to a parched land. Songs to control nature. Power songs.

Songs of a pul.

Whatever signs they'd experienced in their childhood came to this: either now or at some point in the future, they would walk the path of the shaman. And this wouldn't be the last time they would partake of the magic of the desert's beckoning, pale white plant.

For these few, as their minds cleared, they might take the measure of the assembled shamans. They were a strange, possessed lot, their gaze shifting from dreamily distant to intensely piercing, flashing with power. And madness?

There was more to a desert initiation. Though the time sequence is unclear, there were tests of strength, foot races, and an ordeal enduring the stinging of crawling red ants, who were then whipped from a young man's body with nettles. "Ants were supposed to be good because they ate all sorts of plants and got the goodness out of them. Then the ant put the goodness into you when it stung you."[11]

Either before the kikisulem/toloache ceremony or in the weeks following, a ground painting—a symbolic depiction of a clan's cosmology—would be drawn and explained.

The ground painting's lessons learned, it would be swept away—with a possible exception.

A Badlands Mystery Site

Descending from the Santa Rosa Mountains, an ancient cairn-marked trail beckons the eye and foot into badlands of the western Sonoran desert, where there are more cairns, six of them, on the slope of an unnamed dry wash. They lead to a mesa—and end at a fifteen foot diameter rock-lined circle. Within it, there are more rocks, a jumble of them in no discernable order. One wonders: could they once have formed concentric circles—or perhaps a spiral—but then have been since scattered by wind, rain, and time? Both forms were meaningful to shamans.

Whatever the site's intent, it was clearly a work of the hand of man.

Bonnie and I were to puzzle this, and a week later we returned with the wherewithal to map the site—a home-made contraption with the ability to take a straight-down photograph of a plot twenty-five feet across.

From this aerial perspective, there was nothing, really, to suggest concentric circles or a spiral. But, not to give up, we noted four outlying rocks oriented to the cardinal directions. And we tentatively marked connections between rocks that might form lines or curves.

Alignments materialized, yet we were unsure.

11 Florence C. Shipeck, *Delfina Cuero: Her Autobiography*, p. 40.

Above: Beyond a cairn, a trail. *Below:* Marked by orange flags, more cairns in the badlands—leading up to a rock circle site.

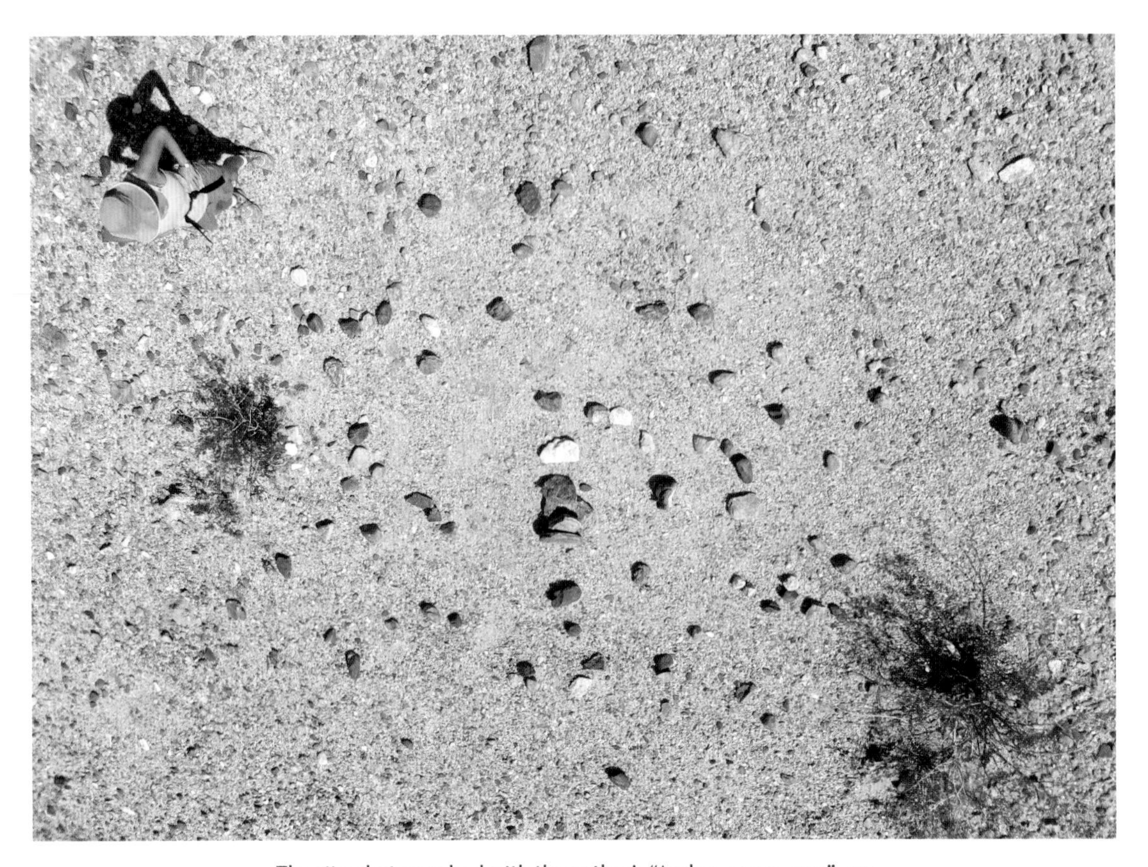

The site photographed with the author's "Archaeo-aero-cam"—an extended pool-cleaning pole fitted with a tripod head. A cable relayed the image to a battery-power television monitor at the base of the pole.

Was what we were seeing a trick of the mind, an attempt to force meaning to a random arrangement? We couldn't really say, and the site might forever have been a mystery had it not been for the field research of one T.T. Waterman, a student of Berkeley's Alfred L. Kroeber.

In the late 1910s, Waterman lived with the Kumeyaay, their territory to the south and west of that of the Cahuilla. He was intrigued by their ground paintings, or rather recollections of them, for their role in initiations had been abandoned when the Kumeyaay were proselytized by Catholic missionaries some fifty years earlier. Hazily at first, Manuel Lachusa, a ninety-year old elder of the settlement of Santa Ysabel,

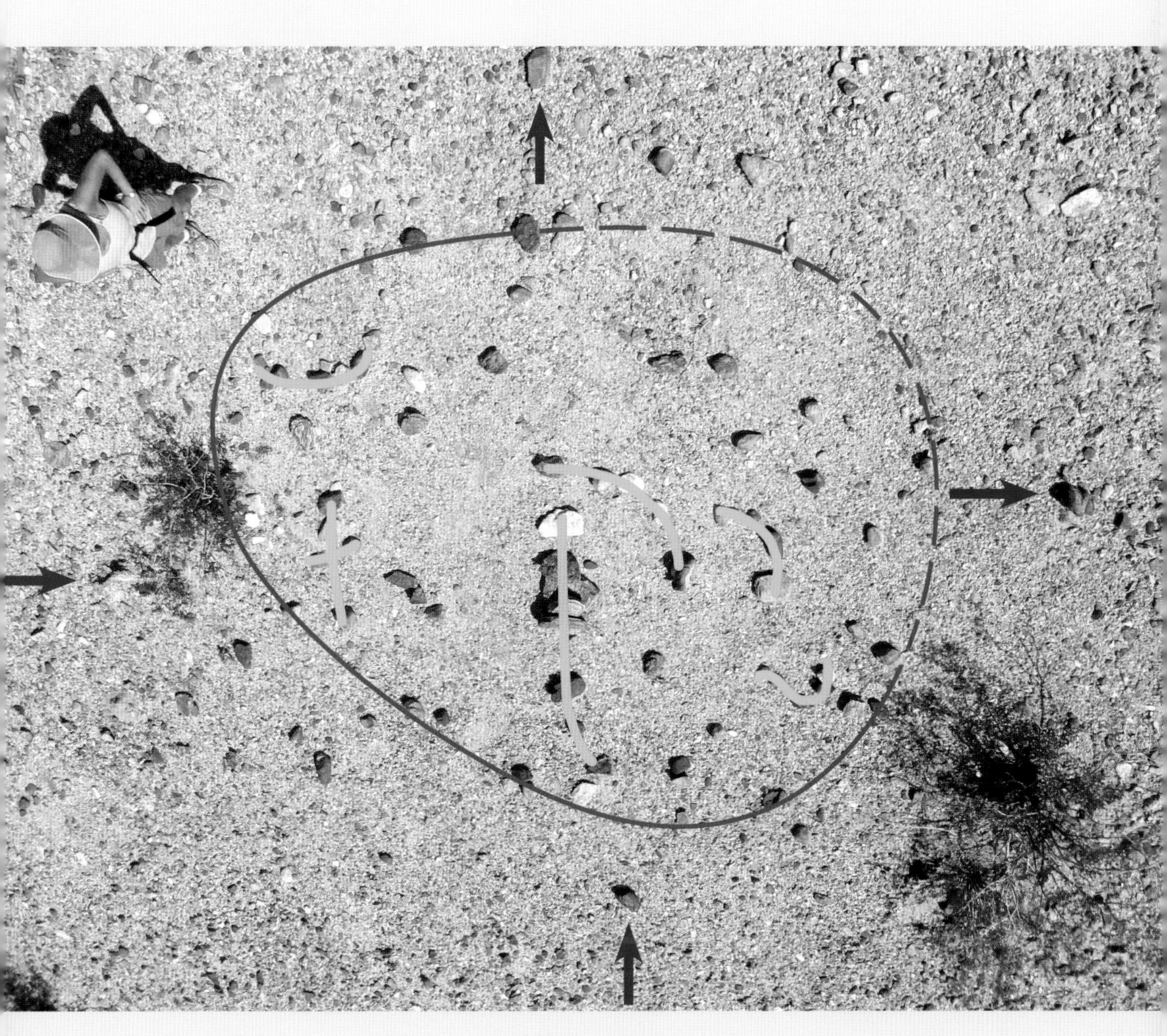

Ancient connections?

At first you see nothing, but then a circle. A T.T. Waterman photograph of Kumeyaay elder Manuel Lachusa. As this petroglyph had faded, so had his memory of past initiation circles.

recalled that a circle depicted the horizon of a tribe's world, and had something to say about sacred animals and stars. The design, he said, was typically 15–18 feet across (the same as our badlands circle!), and encompassed by representations of three outlying peaks and Santa Catalina Island—the far reaches of Kumeyaay territory.

There was more to the circle, Lachusa now remembered. There were animals; there were stars.

Waterman uncapped his pen, listened intently, and with Lachusa looking over his shoulder and making corrections, filled in a circle and numbered its features. There was a trio of spirit helpers: wolf (6), bear (8), and mountain lion (9). As well, there were four species of snakes, from the harmless gopher (14) to the deadly rattler (5). In common, far western desert tribes believed sacred snakes to be guardians of the underworld, protectors of earthen sources of water, fertility—and life.

In addition, clusters of tiny circles portrayed constellations that Europeans recognized as the Pleiades (7), Orion (16), Aquila (15), and Scorpio (11). The Milky Way was somewhere in a ground painting, but try as he might, the old man couldn't place it.

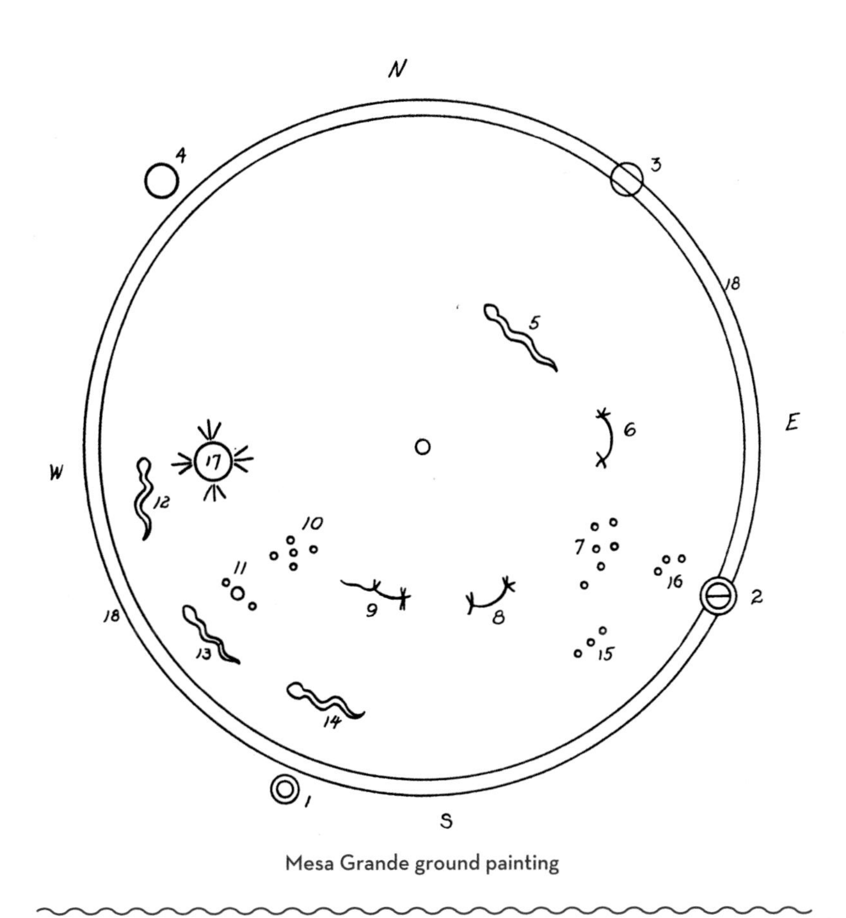

Mesa Grande ground painting

Seven miles distant, at Mesa Grande, the problem was solved in a ground painting recalled by Antonio Maces and Jo Waters.

To these elders, the Milky Way (6)—to the Kumeyaay, the "Ghost Road"—was the design's dominant feature, a central bar flanked by two (of four) sacred snakes. Further, the men drew Waterman's attention to a circle (2) at the west end of their Ghost Road: *a toloache mortar*. The painting, then, would have been made in the course of an initiation in which shamans offered boys drug-induced visions.[12]

And so it was that, with insights documented by T.T. Waterman, our badlands rock circle began to make sense. Granted that there is a difference in that compacted desert pavement and rocks were the media, not sand and paint. This, indeed, could be a prime example of a native

12 Note the differences in the circles made by neighboring settlements. Though sharing common themes, initiations varied not only from tribe to tribe, but from clan to clan.

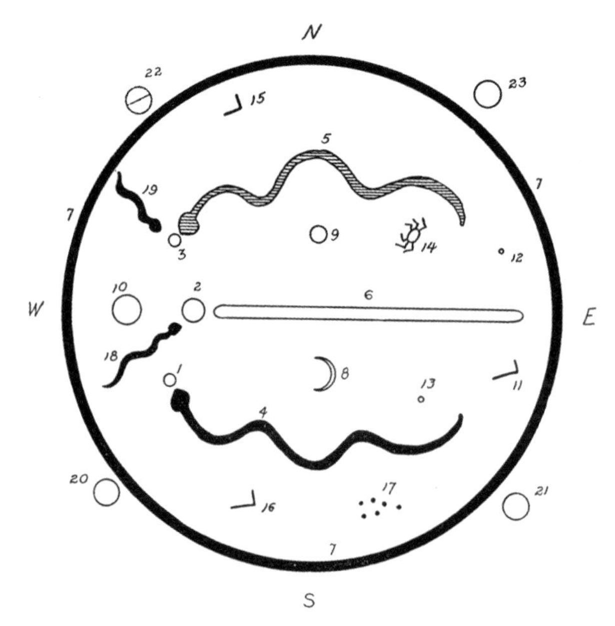

Santa Ysabel ground painting

A possible interpretation of the badlands rock circle.

American penchant for making do with what's handy—what nature offers—and integrating a ceremony with the lay of the natural world.

One could imagine a band of initiates camped here, awaiting nightfall and the grand illumination of their Ghost Road, a road of stories, life lessons, and the answer to where their people came from and where they will go when they die.

The rock circle's major feature—a south-to-north curve incorporating a cairn-like pile of rocks—would appear to be the Ghost Road. The identification is bolstered by a white stone in the same position as a circle

Arcing over the desert sky, the Ghost Road.

(2) in the Santa Ysabel ground painting—*both* symbolic of a toloache mortar (and attendant kikisulem/datura use).

Now, as did T.T. Waterman a century ago, we could—tentatively—fill in the badlands circle.

Accurately aligned south to north in the circle, the Ghost Road appears to be a dividing line. To the east, animals are depicted. Four nested curves stand to be the four sacred snakes of both Santa Ysabel and Mesa Grande. There's also an intriguing "L", a possible symbol of a mountain lion, bighorn sheep or similar spirit helper. (Note that an "L," identified as an *Awik* animal symbol, was thrice used in the Mesa Grande ground painting.)

The western half of the circle looks to be a sky chart, and a remarkably accurate one at that, with constellations placed in proper relation to each other and the Milky Way/ Ghost Road.

To the desert tribes, the sky spoke. The stars looked down and told their stories. Shamans were versed in their language, and recounted . . .

How Moon fled her creator-father . . .

How brash, stupid Coyote attempted to climb a rope to the heavens, and fell to earth . . .

How certain stars are souls of the Chiefs of the First People . . .

And finally, there is the saga of the origin of the First People in the constellation we know as the Pleiades, but that the Cahuilla knew as the "Heart of the World." This was where the First People were born, and where they awaited the completion of the Ghost Road. In time, they traveled to the Ghost Road via the North Star, and in a great journey followed it south.

They then descended to the earth, where they currently dwell.

And when an individual dies, his soul flies to the sky, to become a star in the Ghost Road.

The Pleiades of classical culture.

The "Heart of the World."

And at some point in an ongoing great journey, *all* the Cahuilla—and all the desert's tribes—will leave our earth, ascend to the sky, and follow the Ghost Road back to the "Heart of the World," there to await a new cycle of creation.

White Men and Their Horses

Sweeping and spectacular, the view from the rock circle's mesa is little changed since the days of ancient initiations.[13] But then, if any Cahuilla had been about on a bitterly cold day in December of 1775 AD, they would have been puzzled, even alarmed by a great plume of dust rising just a few miles to the south—rising from a procession of strangely-dressed men and women, their horses, and nearly a thousand head of cattle.

California's first white settlers had set out from northern Mexico, crossed the Colorado River, and traveled this way, with their goal the founding of a colony to the north—San Francisco.

The expedition's leader, Juan Bautista de Anza respected and honored the desert's Indians and, camped by the Colorado River, had struck up what was to become a life-long friendship with the Quechan's Chief Palma. Father Pedro Font, the expedition's joyless, pious chaplain, was of a different opinion. He saw the Quechan to be hopelessly primitive, abysmally godless. "In religion they recognize no special idolatrous cult, although it appears there are some wizards, or humbugs, and doctors among them, who exercise their office by yelling, blowing, and gestures."[14] Hence a first, derisive description of desert shamans.

13 A pre-1500 AD date is likely for circle's creation. Shortly thereafter, a nearby, enormous lake—Lake Cahuilla—was to dry up. And the Cahuilla, no longer able to fish its waters, were to favor more hospitable desert lands.
14 Pedro Font, "The Colorado Yumans in 1774," p. 249.

At daybreak: a man on horseback, possibly of the Anza expedition.
Western Sonoran Desert.

But what, one could ask, might be a shaman's regard for the portly little man in the brown robes and big hat? As a priest Father Font could beseech saints and the Virgin, and fervently pray to God. He could make the sign of the cross in the air and chant endless *Alabados*, hymns in praise of the sacrament.

But beyond beseeching divine succor, could a Catholic priest *make* things happen, could he influence the forces of nature? Even control them?

A shaman could.

Or so he and his people believed.

At the Edge of the Village

SINCE BIRTH, perhaps even before, there had been signs—confirmed now, in a rite of initiation, by the appearance and song of a spirit helper. A young man was destined to become a shaman.

Often, he'd be ambivalent about this, aware that a shaman's life offered power, but at a price of social isolation, privation, and torment. Yet he dared not reject the spirit's entreaty, for to anger the creature was to court death. "Later, when I'm older," he might promise himself. He could—and many did—opt to become a shaman in his forties and fifties.

Quite a number had no choice. They would belong to a family run to shamans, and a father or uncle would set them on the path. Insist on it.

Answering the call, a young man would be drawn to the haunt of one or several shamans, often at a rock art site at the edge of a camp or village. He'd be nervous, even scared.

Wary of its power, normal people avoided the place. They hastened quickly by.

From a nearby outcrop the oasis and village site of Corn Springs.
Southern Mojave Desert.

Corn Springs's erupting granite offered sheltering overhangs and niches, and a grand—if somewhat bewildering—array of petroglyphs.

Sites like this—call them magic mountains—at once beg and defy interpretation. Were their petroglyphs pecked by shamans? Do they depict aspects of a shaman's secretive life and work? Is there a bottom to top—an earth to sky—thematic progression?

Seeking enlightenment, the young man would softly call or whistle like a bird. If a shaman was in a trance, he mustn't be awakened, for his soul might have left his body, and stranded in an alien world, be unable to return.

Should that shaman die, one or more of his spirit helpers would seek vengeance.

The young man might be startled as his call and whistles were answered—as eerie echoes.

But then, from up on this magic mountain, a shaman would respond, and invite the young man to his "cache," his chosen platform or niche. The shaman would question him. Was he prepared for years of training that would severely test his mettle? Even push him to the brink of death? Though he might materially prosper (it was a good living), he would

A puzzling Corn Springs panel.

to the end of his days be a man apart, not exactly an outcast, but a man regarded with a mix of respect, suspicion, and fear. Parents would warn little children not to trail after him, lest his guardian spirits bedevil them.

Was he ready for that?

If the young man professed he was ready for that, other shamans might be summoned and a clan's headman consulted. If they nodded in assent, training would commence.

As the shaman's world was a secret world, little has been revealed of exactly what a candidate was taught, or how his initiation varied from tribe to tribe. There are hints of ritual purifications at desert waterfalls and springs. There would also have been physical tests and ordeals. And a shaman-in-training would be advised to take full measure of the desert, and understand its interplay between its plants and animals, its clouds and shadows, its bright day and mystic levels of darkness, especially "shining darkness."

He might learn an esoteric language, mumbo-jumbo to common folk, but lending shamans an air of superiority as they conversed one to another.

The candidate's achievements, he would be coached, would be all the more admired—and effective—if performed with a theatrical air. Tricks helped. A shaman could swallow a long strand of rawhide, wedging its upper end in his teeth. At a dramatic moment in a shadowy ritual, he could then pull and cough up the now-swollen strip, apparently regurgitating his intestines. And survive.

Hovering on the brink of death, older shamans related, was often their lot, for only by ritually dying could a shaman take leave of the natural world in favor of another.

To that end, a major factor was what the older shamans did not teach, *could not teach*. There were songs and ceremonies—and power—that could only be taught and granted by otherworldly spirit helpers. For this, a shaman-in-training would be on his own.

So it was that he would take leave of his clan and village, and wandering the desert, search out "the dark hole on the cliff," a cave. He would have been told to . . .

> . . . Enter the cave without fear. Inside you will meet a "dream helper." You may see an animal, bird, or mysterious person . . . even a light. Do not fear your helper. It has a present for you, and answer to a question. Reach out and take your gift. Trust your helper and thank it for coming along.

That was the advice of Cahuilla shaman Ruby Modesto.[15]

Further, firsthand recollections of the experience were gathered by Berkeley-trained Willard Z. Park. Dwelling among the Paiute of western Nevada, he earned the trust of several of the tribe's still-active shamans.

In Dick Mahwee's chosen cave,

> I tried to go to sleep. It was hard to sleep there. I heard all kinds of noises. I could hear all the animals. There were bears, mountain lions, deer, and other animals. They were all in caves in the mountain.[16]

Drifting asleep, Mahwee dreamt of a curing ceremony on down the mountain—that failed:

> Patient had died and the people began to cry. . . .
>
> After a while the rock where I was sleeping began to crack like breaking ice. A man appeared in the crack. He was tall and thin.

15 Ruby Modesto and Guy Mount, *Not for Innocent Ears*, p. 89.
16 This and the following Paiute quotes are from Willard Z. Park, *Shamanism in Western North America*, pp. 27–29.

> He had the tail-feather of an eagle in his hand. He said to me, "You are here. You have said the right words. You must do as I tell you. Do that or you will have a hard time. When you doctor, you must follow the instructions that the animals give you."

It is of interest that it is not a single spirit helper that the apparition proposes, but many, each with a singular power. One might aid in curing an arrow wound, another might enable a shaman to charm game, a third could grant him the power to foretell the future. It was a shaman's goal to acquire as many of these as possible. Back in his clan's village a normal person would have only one spirit helper, revealed at the time of his or her coming of age initiation. A shaman might have a dozen or more. Each granting their power—enhancing his role as a "man of power."

Paiute Happy Dave was less blessed. His friend Dick Mahwee recalled that he also went to a cave,

> But he did not want to go inside. A lizard ran up one arm and down the other. Then the wind came up. It blew very hard. Later the owl came and talked to Happy Dave. Told him that he had not done the right thing and that he was wasting his time. Told Happy Dave to go home.

To the south, by the Colorado River, Quechan shaman Manuel Thomas was gathered up by "Shining Darkness," an ethereal, white-winged spirit. "He lifted me by the small of the back and took me through the air." He taught Manual a song to cure a patient:

Your heart is good.
Shining Darkness will be here.
You think only of sad unpleasant things,
You are to think of goodness
Lie down and sleep here

Shining Darkness will join us
You think of this good in your dream
Goodness will be given to you
I will speak for it, and it will come to pass
It will happen here
I will ask for your good
It will happen as I sit by you
It will be done as I sit here in this place.[17]

One can have strange, magical dreams in the desert, stranger yet if they come in a cave of shadowy shapes. Outside an owl hoots and a distant coyote howls. The wind rises, often violently so, with a whirlwind a dream portal to where animals spoke, changed to people and back, and became one with a shaman's soul. The Cahuilla believed that a spirit helper—a *teyawa*—would physically dwell in a shaman's body, a hidden vessel of power from the supernatural world.

No one could say how long it took to school a shaman. For Paiute Dick Mahwee, "In about six years I had received enough instructions to begin a cure." Others claimed that a single, intense trance sufficed.

Sooner or later a new shaman would be tested. Older shamans and tribal elders would gather to witness a cure. They'd pronounce it—and the prospective shaman—a success or failure.

Or they might demand a more strenuous, even dangerous trial. It had to do with dreams, and the belief that only by dying in the everyday world could a shaman be transported to a supernatural one.

He faced: Death . . . then a surreal, fantastic journey . . . and at its end, a re-awakening.

"Do this . . . Show us. Die to live!"

The new shaman, chanting, would dance in the darkness, and fall into a trance. Lit by a flickering fire, he would writhe, suffer torments,

17 Quoted in C. Daryll Forde, *Ethnography of the Yuma Indians*, p.190.

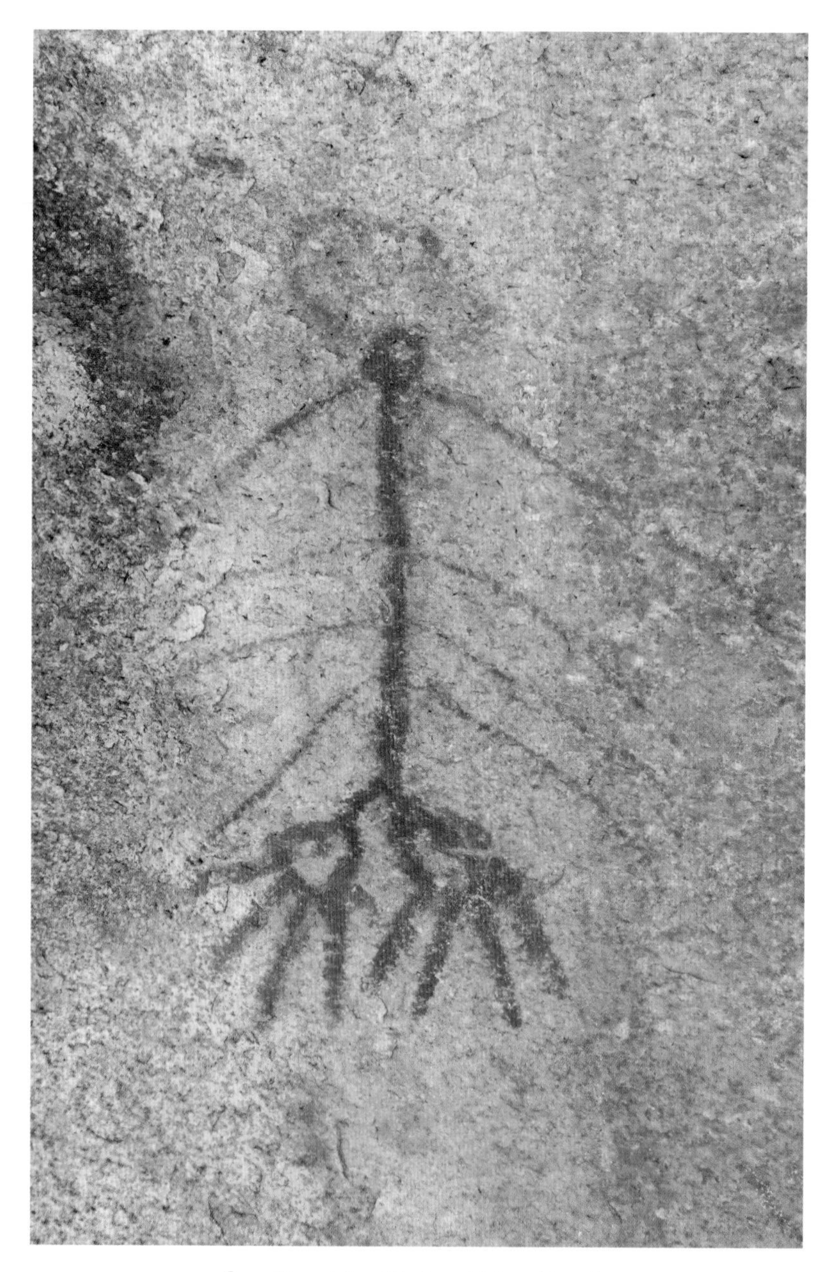

Coso Mountains. Western Mojave Desert.

shout and weep. One or more older shamans would fill common folk in on what—in the young man's mind—was happening. Sinking to the ground, he would be "killed by spirits . . . ghosts." They would tear away his flesh, then one by one, crack his bones.

His skeleton dismembered, the phantoms would disembowel his organs.

"Look! His intestines! He's pulling them out his mouth." The crowd would gasp, stricken with wonder.

Rising on hands and knees, the new shaman would tremble and cry out. Not with words, but with growls and howls. Animal sounds. A good sign, the older shamans explained: he was in the hands of spirit helpers, who would share their knowledge of songs and rites, and lend him their power.

In time, sometimes a very long time, the man's cries and writhing would diminish.

He would cease to breathe (or so it appeared). Had he died? The crowd would hush. And wait. And then, almost imperceptibly, the new shaman would twitch. His eyelids would flutter, and slowly he'd regain his strength. Haltingly, he'd rise to his feet, and accept the accolade of his clan.

The next morning, he would set out to collect a number of power objects essential to his calling. And he'd have his wife or relatives craft his headdress and sew his ritual tunic, different than all others.

His dreams had instructed him in this.

Medicine bags. Little Petroglyph Canyon, western Mojave Desert.

Paraphernalia and Regalia

"A MAN DREAMS THAT a spirit of a deer, eagle, or bear comes to him," recalled Paiute shaman Nick Dowington, "The spirit tells him that he is to be a doctor. . . . The spirit tells him to collect eagle feathers, wild tobacco, a stone pipe, a rattle, and other things. When he gets these things he becomes a doctor."[18]

For fellow shaman Dick Mahwee, his spirit's instructions were:

> I have this feather in my hand. You must get feathers like it. Get dark beads. Put them on the quills of the feathers and tie a strip of buckskin to the quills. Also get the hoof of a deer, and down from an eagle. With these you can go to people to cure them. These are your weapons against sickness.[19]

18 Quoted in Willard Z. Park, *Shamanism in Western North America*, p. 23.
19 *Ibid*, p. 28.

In the phenomenon of *triboluminesence*, a mechanical shock triggers a photon flash.

In some accounts, these were presents offered a shaman by his spirit helper. More the case, the shaman was given a spiritual shopping list, and he then scoured the desert in search of his specified power objects. The assortment varied from tribe to tribe, and from shaman to shaman. A Shoshone might seek the pelts or talons of his spirit helper; a Chemehuevi would be on the lookout for a *poro*, a crooked, wand-like staff. Quartz crystals were universally treasured. In darkness, a shaman could strike two together and with a magical flash of light, release their apparent supernatural power.

A shaman's accumulated objects were tucked away in his medicine bag. Often sewn of badger or weasel skin, it was carried about by a wooden handle.

In his dream state, guided by a spirit helper, a shaman would have visualized his costume, his regalia: a headdress, a neckpiece or cape, and a sack-like animal skin tunic. Add face and body paint, and the effect was impressive, even startling, enough to silence little children—and on one occasion, a brass rail of woozy tipplers in a frontier saloon.

Shoshone Bill Kawitch Has His Picture Taken

In or about the year 1908, the door of the Oasis Saloon in Tonopah, Nevada, swung open. The barkeep blinked at the rush of bright light. His customers, each elbowing the next, turned to behold a strange barefoot figure, half-naked, topped with a feathered cap: a ritually dressed, Shoshone shaman, come to a mining town from who knows where off in the desert.

The man may have uttered a few words of pidgin English, or pantomimed the reason for his appearance. Or the barkeep may have figured this out for himself, and directed the shaman to the rickety stair leading to the second floor studio of photographer E.W. Smith.

All manner of folk sought Smith out: little girls fancying themselves ballerinas, gaunt-faced miners, *doves du prarie* from the Redlight district across the way, even the odd bad man. Chances were that Smith, a kindly fellow with a flowing beard and a like sense of humor, would have taken the shaman in stride, prepared a wet plate, uncapped his lens, and made an exposure.

Smith had a knack for putting his subjects at ease—cajoling them if need be—and then in a second or two, capturing the essence of their personalities. They'd smile, they'd laugh, they'd beam with pride. Or, if a man's demeanor was irresolutely stern and dignified, Smith would make the best of that. Such was the case with his visiting shaman.

The back of the photograph is inscribed: "Shoshone Bill Kawitch."

This rare (and only recently surfaced) image bears examining. What is striking is the shaman's bird-like aspect. His neckpiece is feathered, as is his headdress with its topknot suggestive of that of a quail. His short, decorative skirt appears to be woven of feathers. His shaman's shirt is missing.

Shoshone Bill Kawitch must have been pleased by the image, for he returned accompanied by his wife—and now saw fit to wear his shaman's shirt, emblem of his calling. And he holds a curing feather in his right hand.

What is interesting now is that *his entire regalia has parallels in the desert's rock art.*

Little Petroglyph Canyon, western Mojave Desert.

Left in the top photograph: figure A.
To the right: figures B and C.

In Little Petroglyph Canyon, a few ranges south of Tonopah in the Coso Mountains, there is a wall where one can imagine a scattering of shamans settled in their niches, and lost in their dreams—dreams that on awakening inspired their creation of strange, otherworldly figures.

There was a time, and not that long ago, when such apparitions were considered gods encountered in the visions of shamans, to be worshipped and honored as were deities worldwide. But there is the question: Did not the desert tribes, in the misty dawn of their mythology, either dismiss or kill off their creators? With their function and power preempted by shamans?

In this light, it now appears that the intent of the Little Petroglyph Canyon figures was not to portray long-forsaken gods, *but to portray shamans themselves—in altered, dream states.*

Consider the similarities between the design of the three selected petroglyphs and shaman Shoshone Bill Kawitch's regalia:

- To varying degree, figures A, B, and C are pecked with the zig-zag patterns of Kawitch's shirt.
- Figure B's skirt is identical to Kawitch's.
- Figure B as well has quail-like topknots—mirrored in Kawitch's crested feather headdress. Further, with their clawed feet, all three petroglyphs are bird-like.[20]
- Take note of the faces, and their absence of human features and expression. Figure A hardly has a face at all, only weirdly bulging eyes and a suggestion of hair. B and C are devoid of earthly features and expression.

In an earlier told story of desert creation (pages 12–13), there is an earth-scraped geoglyph that mirrors the face of figure B. As described

20 As we shall see in the chapter "Pursuit of a Lost Soul," flight—magical flight—was essential to a shaman's calling

by an elderly Kwaaymii chief, it was charged with power—the power tirelessly sought by shamans.

In a further pairing, figure C's face radiates power lines similar to those of a sun in a Kumeyaay cave (opposite page).

Little Petroglyph Canyon is rife with such faces and figures. Very few are identical. This stands to reason if each represents not a god, but an individual shaman.

Chances are that the shaman Shoshone Bill Kawitch, somewhere in the Nevada desert, had pecked such an image. It would have come to him in his dream world, and inspired his regalia. It's doubtful that the

The concentric circles of figure B's face mirror those of a western Sonoran desert geoglyph. There is even a semblance of the geoglyph's central pile of magical quartz cobbles.

A telling match: *above*, figure C's face;
below, a sun in a Kumeyaay cave

patrons of Tonopah's Oasis Saloon took him seriously; his appearance would have almost surely prompted crude jibes and slurred jokes. No matter. Bill Kawitch's headdress, shirt, and skirt, as well as the unseen contents of his medicine bag, granted him dignity, respect—*and power*. Power heedless of snickering whites; power awing his fellow Shoshones.

The power of old magic.

A child of the late 1800s.
Top right: A Cahuilla dwelling

Doctoring

PRIOR TO THE COMING of the white man, the desert tribes of the far West enjoyed remarkably good health. Scourges of measles and smallpox were unknown. Clear air, dry heat, and isolation were tonics to muscles, bones, and good spirits. Everyday life was generally ordered and calm, at one with a timeless round of seasons.

Even so, there was illness.

A child could be stricken and her parent sufficiently worried enough to send for a *tingavish*—a practitioner, often an older woman, knowledgeable in the curative power of a variety of plants and herbs. Yerba buena could bring down a fever, and creosote drew out poisons and could heal an infection. The juice of nightshade salved burning eyes; when chewed or smoked, sagebrush alleviated a headache; steeped wild rose doctored a "clogged stomach." The list went on to include sixty or more botanicals. As needed, potions would be mixed and poultices applied—or, in one startling procedure, the patient shamed. If a child was given to fits, Cahuilla healer Ruby Moreno chuckled as she recalled a "fast cure. You just drop your pants and piss on them. They'll be so disgusted with themselves that they will never do it again. I've seen that work."[21]

A sick child might rally, but then relapse, to complain all the more of aches and pains.

But then, by good fortune, magic might be in the air. Hovering nearby, a charmed creature—a hummingbird or even a fly—might take note of the situation, and hasten to a shaman's dwelling, even if hours distant. The messenger would, the Cahuilla believed, alert him as to the whereabouts of the sick child, and even signal if the child might live or die.

Meanwhile, the condition would worsen. The child would cry, sweat, burn with fever. Her parents would be beside themselves. To them illness of this sort wasn't a temporary state from which the daughter stood to recover. It was a prelude to death.

A night would pass, and well before the first, faint glimmer of light on the eastern horizon, the girl's father would be on his way to summon a shaman. Sunrise was considered the ideal time for this.

And there would be times, it was reported, that the father met the shaman hastening the other way. He knew. Even so, lighting his pipe, he would affect an aloofness as he considered the man's plea. In due time, a fee would be set or a gift promised. There was a time when beads, skins, blankets and horses secured a shaman's services. In the early 1900s, three to five dollars were charged. A guarantee might be offered. If the patient died, the shaman would waive all, or at least some, of his fee.

In an aside, the shaman might claim that his fees were set by spirit helpers; free services, he asserted, would anger them, turn them on him, threaten his life. As if his calling wasn't dangerous enough. Nevertheless, in one shaman's words,

21 Ruby Modesto and Guy Mount, *Not For Innocent Ears*, p. 51.

> "Always, I think, I have been asked to cure when I felt strong for it, and on these occasions I am always successful. . . . I have a different [special] feeling. . . . There is a fluid in me which I have drawn from the air and I do not mind walking a great distance."[22]

He might stop in his tracks, though, if he spied a coyote or owl or heard their cry carried in the desert air. They were spirit messengers—bearing word that his new client had faded and died. He'd not be needed.

Barring an ill omen, a shaman would typically delay his arrival until an hour or so after dark. And often, he would be accompanied by an assistant, his interpreter or "talker." On entering a client's home, he would be on the alert for a whiff of frog or fox, evidence that a malign spirit hovered in the air.

The shaman would slip off his moccasins or sandals. If he hadn't already, he would dab his face and body with dots and lines of red and white pigment. Directing the patient be turned so that her head pointed south, he would seat himself and, with words and song unintelligible to family and friends sitting on their heels and lining the wall, address whatever spirit was responsible for the ailment. His talker would supply a running commentary:

> Our doctor is here. He is a good doctor. He is a strong doctor. You are poisoning this girl. The doctor will find out about you. He knows you. Go away and leave this girl alone. Go away and do not come back again![23]

Withdrawing his bone pipe from his medicine bag, the shaman would light it with an ember from the fire.

22 Quoted in C. Daryll Forde, *Ethnography of the Yuma Indians*, p. 184.
23 Quoted in Willard Z. Park, *Shamanism in Western North America*, p. 50.

Or he might demonstrate his power by grasping a coal and popping it in his mouths.

He would then "smoke" the girl, cloud her with breaths to purify her.

He would then settle back, continue to thoughtfully smoke, and sing himself into a trance. No one would dare speak or murmur or cough; this could harm the shaman, who in his mind had entered a realm of darkness, not darkness as anybody else knew it, but "darkness as a second night." *Shining darkness*—a magical darkness that could seek out and reveal the presence of a malign spirit. To gauge the spirit's power—versus his—the shaman might visualize his patient in a field of flowers. She'd

Ambrosio Castillo, a Cahuilla fire-eater.

pick them and if they were fresh, she would soon be up and about. If the flowers were withered, she would likely die. If she walks away and leaves no footprints, she would certainly die and was beyond curing.

With his eyes half closed or even rolled up into his head, the shaman sways back and forth. His talker gives meaning to his movements, first relating that he has sought the appropriate spirit helper, but has not yet made contact. The shaman gestures erratically; he jerks about. The good spirit is near, just outside in the desert night. The shaman breaks into song, loud and forceful. The song could be lengthy,[24] or as short as four or five words interspersed with incomprehensible syllables. It could simply be:

> "The spirit pursued. The girl in peace."

To mesmerizing effect, a line like this would be ceaselessly repeated, over and over, with hardly a chance for the shaman to catch his breath. As many as two hundred times, with his body trembling, shaking, the pitch of his voice higher and higher. A desired spirit helper has "come like the wind," the talker explains, and is entering the shaman's body.

The shaman becomes his spirit helper; the spirit helper becomes the shaman. They are one.

Possessed by his spirit helper, the shaman is primed to work his magic. His talker turns to him, to demand:

> "Cure this girl. Make the sickness disappear. Suck out the sickness inside her. Show us the sickness you suck out. Then she will recover."[25]

The shaman does just that.

24 As an example of this, there is the song spirit-dictated to Quechan Manuel Thomas. See p. 48–49.

25 Quoted in Willard Z. Park, *Shamanism in Western North America*, p. 50.

Combating evil power with his own, he might raspily breathe on the patient, or inhale tobacco smoke, fill his mouth with frothed saliva, and spray the potion on the terrified girl. The treatment could then physically escalate. To the accompaniment of "unearthly howling," a shaman might pummel or slap the girl. And there was a doctor of the Desert Cahuilla given to vigorously butting his patients with his head.

With his feathered wand, the shaman might point to the site of the poisoning, then brush the area, be it the girl's stomach, chest, or head. All eyes would be upon him as he now attempted to suck out the disease—manifest as an object—with a bone or willow tube, or most often, his mouth.

Although he would never actually bite or incise a patient, a dark, blood-like liquid would ooze and drip from his lips. All the while, his talker would lead the assembled crowd in repetitive, hypnotic song—until, with a shake of a rattle, the shaman signaled them to stop.

He spits whatever liquid he's sucked into a shallow hole scooped in the earthen floor.

The song continues. The shaman rises, repeatedly stamps his right foot, and dances around the fire, first clockwise, then counterclockwise.

He kneels now, and applies his mouth anew to the sucking. His talker confides to the crowd that the sucking is actually done by the shaman's spirit helper, lodged in his throat. If need be, the dance-sucking cycle is several times repeated, until . . .

The shaman sucks out a malign, offending object. It could be a pebble, a small black lizard, a bird claw, a fish bone, an insect, or worm. Among the Cahuilla, it was said to resemble flakes of snow. In the ceremony's firelight and darkness, it was often difficult to say what it really was, with, at best the crowd catching a hasty glimpse as it was flung in the hole where the shaman had spat, and piled over with dirt.

Addressing the spirit at the root of the illness, the talker would have the final say:

> "You are a weak thing, without power, hasty and heedless of our power. You are evil. Go back to the western sky where you belong. Stay away and do not dare to return."[26]

The ceremony would diminish in intensity as the shaman led family and friends in a concluding dance around the fire. On his signal, they would stop, blow on their arms, and vigorously shake their clothes. If a sickness-inducing spirit was lingering in the home, this would drive it away.

The shaman's magical shining darkness would fade, then the darkness that concealed it. The sun would rise. Greatly relieved, family and friends would part. The girl would sigh with relief, even smile.

Yet, as the shaman and his talker left the dwelling and disappeared off across the desert, there would be a sense of unease.

A spirit had "shot" the girl with a magical foreign object. It had been ritually sought and removed. But who or what had called up the spirit? Summoned it and, to evil end, directed its power?

None but another shaman, it was widely believed. An evil shaman, a sorcerer, with the power at his disposal indifferent as to whether it was used to good or bad intent.

But why harm an innocent child?

A family enemy, out of spite or vengeance, may have paid the shaman-sorcerer to do this. Or, the sorcerer may have become so dissolute in his ways that he couldn't help himself.

By all accounts, sorcerers were legion—and despised—in the desert.

26 Quoted in C. Daryll Ford, *Ethnography of the Yuman Indians*, p.188.

What to make of such shamans? Haughty and scowling. Eyes lidded, yet burning. As an early report had it, "Their snuffy, artful faces are lighted by beady eyes," wrote E.J. Trippel in an 1889 issue of *The Overland Monthly*. Are they men of good or evil intent? The question plagued desert tribes.

Sorcerers

A SUCCESSFUL CURE had its aftermath, often grisly. None but a sorcerer, it was widely felt, could have been responsible for the *magical airshot* that had inflicted a patient's grief. Sometimes, there would be little doubt as to the perpetrator; he might even confess and repent what he'd done, and save his skin. Or he might flee a tribe's territory. Most often, his identity would be uncertain, and to forestall further mischief, low talk and nodded heads would agree: the sorcerer, straight way, must be rooted out and killed.

If identified with reasonable certainty, he'd hardly have a chance; he might not even be aware he'd been implicated.

Awaiting a favorable opportunity, a designated executioner would catch the sorcerer-shaman off-guard. He'd creep up behind him, and before he could resist, kill him. The malign shaman would be stabbed, clubbed, or shot. His corpse would be flung into his dwelling, and the hut set afire and burned to the ground.

Among the Cahuilla, the tale was told of *Met* (Gopher), a shaman-sorcerer dwelling west of Palm Springs.

> Met was a great pul who claimed to be God. He could catch bullets in his hands, and see the child in the sun. He bewitched many people and killed them, so his daughter asked the people to kill him. A bear pul was elected to kill him. It was in summer and the watermelons were ripe; as Met was sitting down eating one of these, he came up behind him and hit him over the head with a digging stick, but he could not kill him. All the other people then piled rocks over Met and finally he died.[27]

Sorcerers died hard. There was one who never did, and from generation to generation, was a figure of fright to wide-eyed Cahuilla children and their elders. His name was *Tahquitz* (or sometimes, *Acquits*).

The Evil Shaman Tahquitz

It was said that when the earth was newly formed and populated, the creator-god Mukat granted a select few of his people special powers. They would be puls. The first was Tahquitz, and he was to endure as the most powerful. As related by Francisco Patencio, the latter-day chief of the Palm Springs Cahuilla:

> He was very wise and knew many things. He said, "You watch me now, because there is no danger." He then took an arrow, pushed it down his throat, then thrust it in his side, then through his head at the temples, then stabbed himself through the lungs. He said, "You can see it is nothing. I am not dead. It is only play."

27 William D. Strong, *Aboriginal Society in Southern California*, p. 169.

One of many caves in boulder-strewn Tahquitz Canyon.

> He was a man of great power. But he did not do any good. He never tried to cure anybody, or do any good for anyone. So he did not have any friends among his people, and he knew that he did not deserve any.
>
> He became a very bad spirit.... He speaks through the lightning and thunder, and is seen everywhere. He kills the people, and the spirits of the people.[28]

Tahquitz, Chief Patencio continued, dwelt up a rocky canyon in the San Jacinto Mountains.

There, he dwelt in a cave under a large rock. There, he learned to fly and assume all manner of clever disguises, which allowed him to inveigle men and women—especially young women—up his canyon. While on their way, the sky would darken and lightning would flash—and Tahquitz would loom, revealed as the monster he truly was. A giant, a demon! He'd kill with a terrible sweep of his hand. Pulling an arm free of it socket, he'd gnaw its still warm flesh. Bones crunched between his teeth; blood oozed from his jaw, ran down his arms, soaked his gnarled hands.

Tahquitz would march on up his canyon—each stomp of his huge feet an echoing peal of thunder—to finish his dinner in his lair.

The Cahuilla believed that the infernal shaman lived on in his haunted canyon. Only the foolhardy would venture up there, to quickly flee at the sound of strange noises reverberating in the mountain—the groans of victims, the roar of the cannibal-demon.

As the Cahuilla's creator-god Mukat had fallen from grace, so had Tahquitz. And although Mukat's people had killed Mukat, they failed to kill Tahquitz. For sorcerers to come, he would be a demonic role model. Quite a number of them, it was said, sought him as a spirit helper.

28 Chief Francisco Potencio, *Stories and Legends of the Palm Springs Indians*, p. 12 and 44.

Witching, the Ways

Sorcerers, as one might expect, were secretive. Even so, from good shamans anxious to expose them, glimpses survive of their craft. Accordingly, it is possible to venture a brief compendium of their maleficence.

IN HIS DREAMS. A sorcerer could concentrate his dark thoughts by day, and by night dream the image of his victim, and in that dream, grasp a sharp stick and impale the victim's heart.

CLOSE CONTACT. A sorcerer could work his magic upon touching a person, handing him food, or, in feigned friendship, offering him a pipe packed with tobacco. When no one was looking, he might sprinkle powdered elephant tree bark on a victim's food, and bitterness would soon rack his body. All the while, there would not be the slightest hint of what the sorcerer was up to.

Anything personal could be used to witch someone—hair from a comb, nail parings, clothing, spittle, or blood. Their whole lives through, Cahuillas would keep these to themselves, or take extraordinary care in their disposal.

Still, a wily sorcerer could scoop sand from a person's footprint, and witch his feet and legs with searing pain.

MAGICAL AIRSHOTS. Playing an eagle bone whistle, a sorcerer would seek out his desert's "poison places," and there, in a basketry tray, sweep up supernatural *airshot*. Exactly what this was is hard to say, for it was invisible. Nevertheless, it was capable—as an arrow—of propelling a disease object into an intended victim's body. The skin wouldn't be broken, but the evil little object would be there—festering and death-dealing—unless and until a benevolent shaman sucked it out.

A good shaman, a curing shaman, would identify airshots as an evil counterpart's weapon of choice. But did the requisite sorcerer, let alone his airshot, *even exist*? That is a very good question in that the sole proof of evil intent was a disease object sucked and spat from the mouth of a man with a living to earn and a reputation to enhance. This could well explain why, in the aftermath of many cures, no evil-doer was fingered, found, killed, or exiled. He could have been cloaked by his malign power, it may have been claimed, but more the case, he was imaginary, a foil in a good shaman's performance.

And that performance, whatever its sleight of hand or tongue, that performance had its effect. Its old magic—compelling and cathartic—prevailed.

FROG SORCERY. This was the worst. Frogs were formidable, near supernatural in their ability to hibernate for years in dried mud, even freeze solid in a cold spell.

Echoing the tale of the demise of the Cahuilla's creator-god Mukat,[29] the excrement of a victim would be obtained, stuffed into a frog's mouth, and the poor creature's mouth pinned shut with thorns. The sorcerer would order: "Go on . . . Eat it!"

"That person would die for sure," Cahuilla medicine woman Ruby Modesto was to lament, "Nothing can be done to counteract frog sorcery."

29 See p. 46

From wishing ill to tormenting frogs, a sorcerer-shaman's courting of evil was a cautionary tale. Innocently enough, he might mix and peddle—for a price—a potion that in the eyes of a sought-after lover, could make the ugliest of men and women be handsome and beautiful, radiantly so. Next, on behalf of an offended or enraged friend or acquaintance, he might be engaged—for a good price—to even the score with whoever had set the man off. The shaman would answer the call of the desert flicker: "Pee-um, pee-um"—"Witch him, witch him!"

He would savor the results, and soon be tangled in a spider web of his own spinning. According to (good) Paiute shaman Joe Green, "After a shaman poisons one person, he cannot stop. Then he always wants to make people sick and kill them." Adds Ruby Modesto, "Some puls were just plain evil. They would poison people just to get rid of them, even in their own family.[30]

The Evil Shaman Tamiotemevie

Sorcerers at the peak of the power, it was believed, would revel in evil beyond measure. Witching up drought or torrential rain, they could wipe out crops. They could conjure an epidemic.

In the face of such power, it could be all hell killing them off.

As was the case with the Cahuilla's Tamiotemevie.

As a casual demonstration of his power, Tamiotemevie would hold his pipe up to the sun, and in a flash, its tobacco would smoke. Or he would reel out his monstrous tongue, as long as a man was tall.[31]

Delighting in distress, Tamiotemevie cruelly abused his wife, until a day came when she'd had enough, and ran off. Tracking her, the sorcerer

30 Quoted in Willard Z. Park, *Shamanism in Western North America,* p. 44; in Ruby Modesto and Guy Mount, *Not for Innocent Ears,* p. 43.
31 A variation on the swallowing rawhide illusion? See p. 46.

Desert masks of death.

was on the verge of capturing and doing terrible things to her, only to be ambushed and seized by brave Cahuilla.

Without hesitation, they killed him—as indeed they had killed him several times before. But each time he had willed himself back, alive and awful as ever. This time, though, they tore him to pieces, little pieces, and were about done with him when a lizard jumped from his heart, a lizard that, as Tamiotemevie's spirit helper, was the source of his power. The Cahuilla chased and killed it; for had they not, it would have put the wicked shaman back together and restored his breath of life.

The Cahuilla buried the lethal little creature deep in the earth. Soon after the earth quaked, the lizard trying to escape its tomb. But it could not.

So it was that Tamiotemivie died. But in legend, the demonic Tahquitz lived—and lives on. In December of 1899, he was credited with a destructive San Jacinto earthquake. As Cahuilla chief Francisco Patencio would have it, he "causes the wrecks of trains and automobiles, and delights in everything that makes people trouble."[32] Ever a master of disguises, he was said to have in broad daylight strolled the hamlet of Palm Springs. Gray-gloved and sporting a fancy cane, he appeared "all same swell white man."[33]

If a meteor flashed low across the night sky, the Cahuilla—especially young women—shuddered and looked away, for that was Tahquitz, ever on the hunt for wandering souls.

32 Chief Francisco Patencio, *Stories and Legends of the Palm Springs Indians*, p. 44.

33 George Wharton James, "The Legend of Tauquitch and Algoot," p.158.

Part Two

DREAM QUEST

Circles and Caves

Badlands in the western Sonoran desert—stark, all but lifeless—have their surprises. As you wander a maze of muted mud hills, the miles and hours drift by. Then, of a sudden, you round a corner and behold a vaulted, inky-blue night sky. It's a natural outcropping, you tell yourself. Nonetheless, above a sleeping, misty blue earth there is a host of constellations and the angled tracks of shooting stars.

There is more. Further along on the outcropping, there's a shaman, arms raised to the sun, and nearby, a needle-toothed serpent.

Man made? Not so. The artist is nature, which raises a question: as Indians lived in harmony with nature, how can one tell what they did or didn't create? The difference can be subtle.

Beyond and above its badlands, the desert's ridges and mesas are dotted by the hundreds with what appear to be cleared circles. Anywhere from three to twelve feet across, they are lighter than the surrounding desert pavement, and are sandy, smoothed out, and vegetation free. They can be sighted on Google Earth.

No one knows exactly what to make of these circles. Did infrequent rainfall long ago create vernal pools? Might they be man-made? The author and his wife have surveyed hundreds, and although we remain somewhat baffled, believe they may have been born of sand excavated by industrious desert ants, then enlarged by larger creatures taking sand baths. Some circles—our guess is one in fifty—were smoothed and rounded by native Americans.

With minimal effort, a natural form could accommodate and serve . . . a shaman? Even a community of shamans?

Though there is tribal lore testifying to their use by shamans, the idea that the circles were ancient dream quest sites has been repeatedly raised—and dismissed. To the contrary, it was claimed, they were remnants of either willow-branch shelters or hunting blinds. But considering their location in open highlands distant from any known water sources, neither argument makes sense. Why live where hauling water is an unavoidable chore? And what game would be so clueless as to wander by?

One feature these circles distinctively share is a serene, often inspiring view of near and distant mountains and valleys. The Quechan, to this day, believe them to have served as shamans' "meditation circles." And in the Quechan territory of Picacho, that role is convincingly confirmed.

On terraces west of the Colorado River, hundreds of circles are clearly man-made. Some have walls as much as a meter high. And repeatedly, clusters of circles are interconnected by paths, not the ordinary Indian footpaths common to the desert, but paths of painstakingly cleared squares.

There is absolutely no *practical* reason for these; their intent and use can only have been *ritual*. Out of sight of the circles, the cleared squares revert to ordinary footpaths—with the exception of paths that leads directly from one cluster of circles to another, in one instance paved with nearly fourteen-hundred squares.

Above: Shamans' circles. Rims of cleared pebbles are telltale signs. *Below:* A circle within a circle—possibly a "shaman's hearth" as a symbolic portal for dream quests. *Right:* Nearby, evidence of an ancient presence—a scattering of shards of a broken pot.

Picacho circles. In the distance, marshes line the Colorado River.

At day's end, one can imagine shamans pacing these steps to their circles, there to raise their arms to the sun, ever a source of power.

Fires would have been kindled in nearby horseshoe-shaped hearths, and "dance lines" of shamans would have moved to the repetitive, trance-inducing beat of one or more drums. As night fell and the moon rose, they would disperse to their individual circles. Not all of the circles would be occupied; it is probable that some were cleared by shamans long dead, and no longer used (as upon his death, a man's house was abandoned or burned to the ground).

There was magic in the circles. They were metaphors for heightened power, and with it, access to the supernatural. So it is that tiny pebble circles are often found within them, and functioned as portals to other worlds, dream worlds, worlds beyond imagining.

Mountain Dream Quest Sites

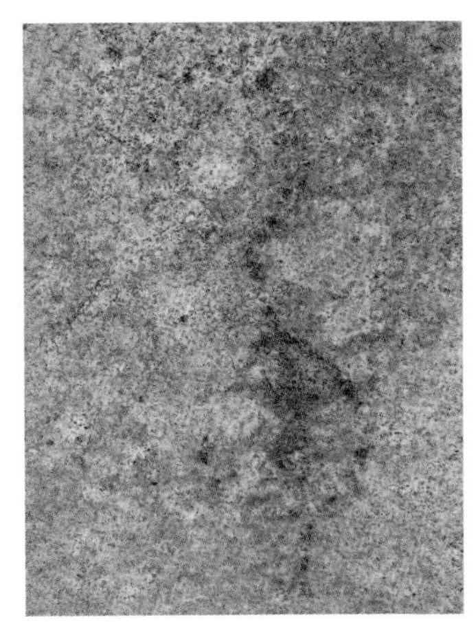

A fading image of a shaman at the edge of a Kumeyaay village site. A double-circle head with radiating power lines is barely visible. Western Sonoran Desert.

Higher in the desert's mountains, a rock niche or cave was a shaman's haunt. It had the power of a cleared circle, perhaps more. Consider now, a shaman who over the years had felt his power wane, and sought to have it renewed. Or he might be set on acquiring more power than ever, and gaining the prestige (and fees) of a shaman outperforming and shaming rival shamans. A "shaman of shamans."

A desert shaman might undertake a dream quest close by his village. Or his cave could be many hours or even days away. This would have been the case with a shaman setting out from a Timbisha Shoshone village—still inhabited—on the floor of Death Valley. If flowing water or a spring was at hand, as at Furnace Creek, he would ritually bathe and purify himself in preparation of the ordeal and trance to come. He would have an eye out for "water babies," nasty little spirits that could bewitch or even drown him. (More on these later.)

The shaman would ascend and cross the Funeral Mountains and then, guided by a series of landmarks, find his way to a rocky draw that led him higher and yet higher until ranges and valleys stretched away in all directions.

A hidden path then traversed the face of a cliff to a rock shelf—and a cave.

There was an elderly Timbisha Shoshoni woman who as a child was taken to the cave, possibly for a doctoring ritual. She was told, "Now you've seen it. Never come back."

Common folk ventured here at their peril, for caves and their power were guarded by supernatural spirits. "Personified fire" was a blindingly bright light that was "a kind of person without legs that just floats along," or in another report, a ghost dog that "had a snake's body and human hands for feet." Shamans took care as they approached their haunts. A supernal light could beckon, or challenge. Spirits could be cranky. The mountain could shake, with boulders pitching over its cliffs. However close they came to crushing him, the shaman would stand firm. It was a test. With more to come.

As the sun arced west and shadows enveloped the site, the shaman would ready himself for his dream quest. It wouldn't be tonight, or even the next night. There was no rush. The time would come when the time came. He would don his ritual skirt, shirt, and headdress. He would assemble his paraphernalia, which he either had brought with him, or hidden away in his cave. There was talk of powerful shamans keeping their magical objects locked away in solid rock, which on their command, would magically offer up pipe and talismans.

Denying himself food and water, the shaman would fast.

He would smoke, even ingest powerful native tobacco, cause for time to stand still, and otherworldly forces prevail.

A coyote would howl in the night. Singing, even shouting, the shaman would answer. Or he might shudder at the muted hoot of an owl, death's messenger. Soon enough, he well knew, he would face death itself. And transcend it?

In the still of the night air, a drum might throb, for a hundred meters on up the mountain, there was a second cave, and a second shaman might well have taken up residence.

The next morning, the shaman would, with great care, unwrap the dried root of a datura plant. Grinding it, he would dissolve it in just the right amount of water, all the while whispering to the root as if it was a sentient being—as indeed were all plants and animals and even rocks.

For a time, a neighboring shaman might join him in a protracted round of drumming and dancing. The beat would echo away on down the canyon.

Shaman's cave. Northern Mojave Desert. The cave is painted with an array of images, including what appears to be a giant grinning, white face, *below*. (Or this could be something else entirely.)

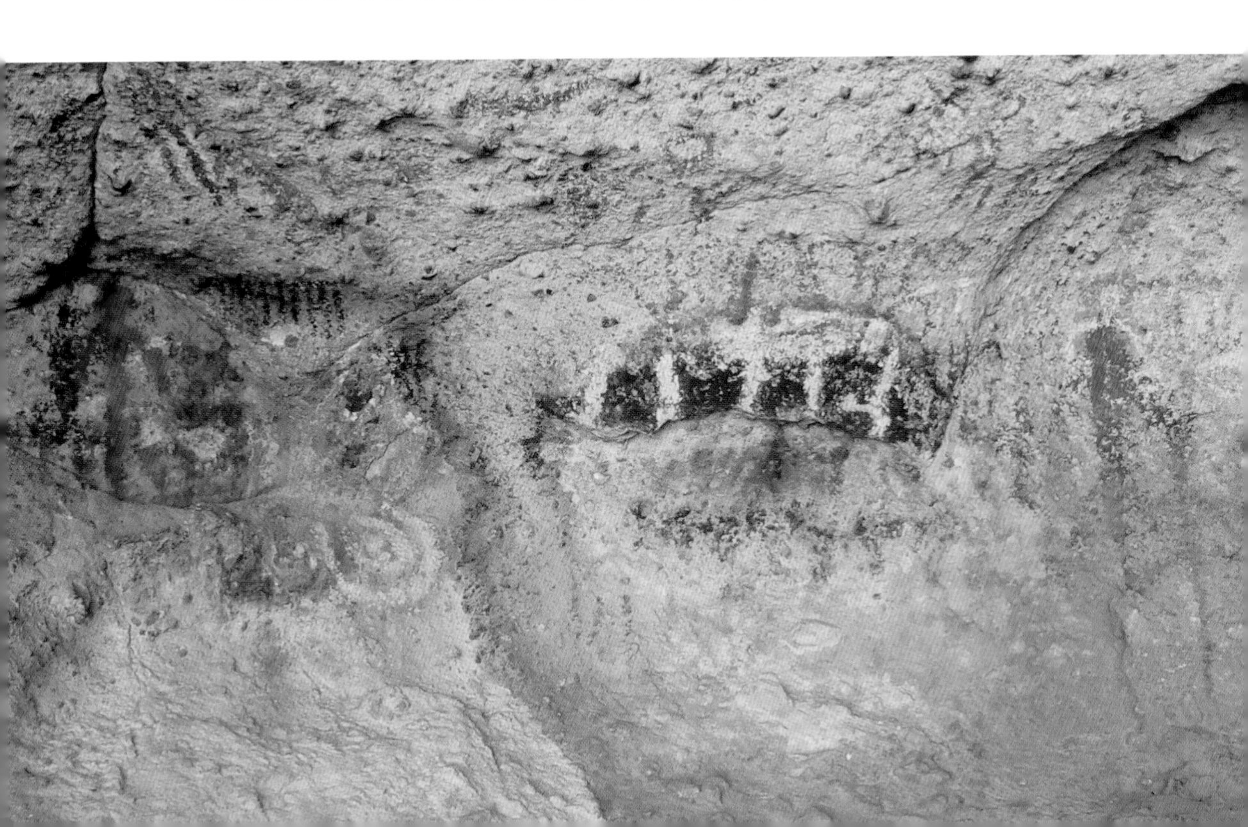

A shaman's self-portrait. His left hand grasps the head of a large lizard, a spirit helper.

Were the spirits listening?

The two shamans would part. They'd soon find out.

At dusk, our shaman would, elbows crooked, raise his arms to the setting sun to expose his "seat of power," his right wrist, to its rays. Watching the stars, one by one, take their place, he would await total darkness, and with it, the "shining darkness behind it." Only then could a dream quest commence, for in the realm of the spirits, everything is reversed. Night becomes day; a parched desert is a verdant forest; dun offal is glittering treasure.

He would swallow his datura, his magical toloache.

He would, faster and faster now, beat his drum.

His skin would weirdly tingle, as if crawling with ants. Then his arms and legs would numb. His face would droop and his jaw slacken. His gaping mouth would dry to the point of burning.

He would try to move, but find nothing solid beneath his feet.

With a loss of muscle control, he would flail, scream, collapse. His pulse would dangerously slow, only to surge as he was racked with wrenching, agonizing convulsions. He would bleed from the nose and mouth; his eyes would roll back.

He would shudder, then twitch; the twitching would cease.

He would die.

(Or so it appeared.)

Still there: rock talismans.

Trances: Taking Leave

THE BEGINNING of a dream quest was hardly an ecstatic experience. It was torment and torture, and at times fatal.

In the theater of his mind, a shaman would be pierced by arrows, torn apart, disemboweled. This was deemed necessary, for only by "dying" in his earthly world could a shaman enter and experience the realm of the supernatural. Whatever bodily chemistry was in play, the shaman believed his self-sacrifice to be a necessary step on a path to transfiguration—and rapture—to come.

Now irreversibly on that path, the shaman would hear things: whining, buzzing, tinkling—aural hallucinations. He'd open his eyes. His vision would be blurred, but then would clear as the rock wall of his cave fractured and cracked open, to reveal before him a long, shadowy tunnel.

The shaman would be lifted in the air, now weightless. As he passed from his cave into the tunnel, he sensed the presence of the spirits of

Above: At the end of a shaman's cave, a natural tunnel. Western Sonoran Desert.
Left: Spirit at entrance of a natural tunnel. Southern Mojave Desert.

spiders or rattlesnakes, guardians of the supernatural, there to scare away anyone unworthy of their realm.

In the dark tunnel, he would hear more than he saw. Hisses. Rattles. Whispers. Roars.

Were insects scuttling in and out of his ears? Spiders spinning webs in his mouth?

Figures at a symbolic portal to another world.
Northern Mojave Desert.

Spiral and grid. Little Petroglyph Canyon, western Mojave Desert.

On and on, he'd float, finally to enter a great miasmic hollow in the earth, the dwelling place of a multitude of animal spirits, jostled by a host of ancestral ghosts, only they weren't in a corporal form one might expect, but rather appeared as a shifting, rising and receding concatenations of wavy lines, dots, and grids. As best he could, the shaman took pains to remember these. Their apparently random forms were important. Magical. Returning to his desert world, he would peck or paint them in or near his cave.

Why the importance of these forms? What was happening here?

For an answer we must momentarily take leave of our shaman—and puzzle his state of mind and perception in the light of recent anthropological breakthroughs. There was a time when these abstract forms, as recorded in rock art, were dismissed as doodles. No longer. Scattered across the desert by the thousands, they have proven key to the understanding of dream quests, not only in North America, but worldwide.

A Theory of Entopic Patterns

In many respects, life in Africa's Kalihari Desert was much the same as in our Sonoran and Mojave deserts—the heat, the elusive game, the San Bushman's struggle to survive. Shamans dwelt at the edge of San villages, and in historic times, described their role in creating rock art, which they freely admitted were a product of hallucinogenic dream quests.

In the early 1970s, the role of drugs in the San's rock art prompted David Lewis-Williams of Johannesburg's University of Witwateersrand to seek a neurophysiological explanation for the art's recurrent, abstract imagery. Working with his student Thomas Dodson, Lewis-Williams believed that the answer was "entopic"—literally, "within the eye." The eye, they believed, is capable of—on its own and independent of outside influences—creating a range of "phosphenes." Dots, squiggles, and the like. And to the researchers' delight, these phosphenes appeared the same one culture to the next, worldwide.

There was, the two researchers believed, nothing all that mystical about what a shaman perceived in the initial stage of a dream quest. Rather, the man was caught up in artifacts of vision—conjured by drugs.[34]

Lewis-Williams and Dodson charted seven basic phosphene patterns.[35]

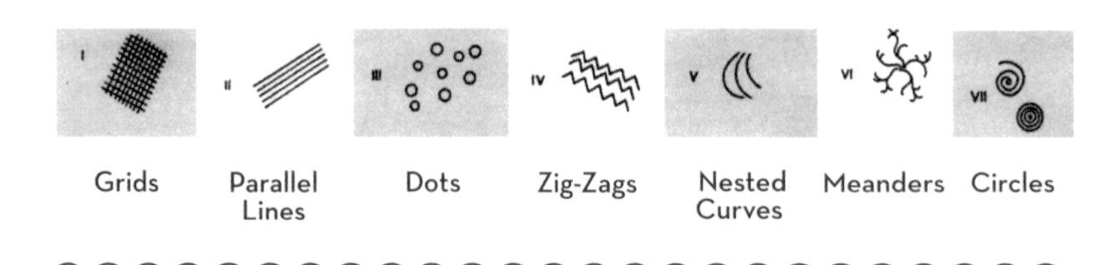

34 For a glimpse of this, close your eyes, gently rub your eyelids, and witness an abstract theater of light. Then imagine the patterns you see run wild in a hallucinatory state.
35 Groundwork for this categorization was laid by Heinrich Kluver, as well as by researchers Kellogg, Knoll, and Kugler.

In California, Ken Hedges of the San Diego Museum of Man and David Whitley of UCLA reconsidered the rock art of the desert West and, with minor variations, discovered and catalogued the very same building blocks. The phenomena, they believed, was hard-wired to the human nervous/optical system.

Here, then, is a phosphene sampler:

Above: Parallel lines.
Below: Dots

Above: Nested curves.
Below: Meanders

Particular import may have been given to meanders. They occur naturally as quartz veining in rocks—rocks that were venerated as the dwelling place of living spirits.

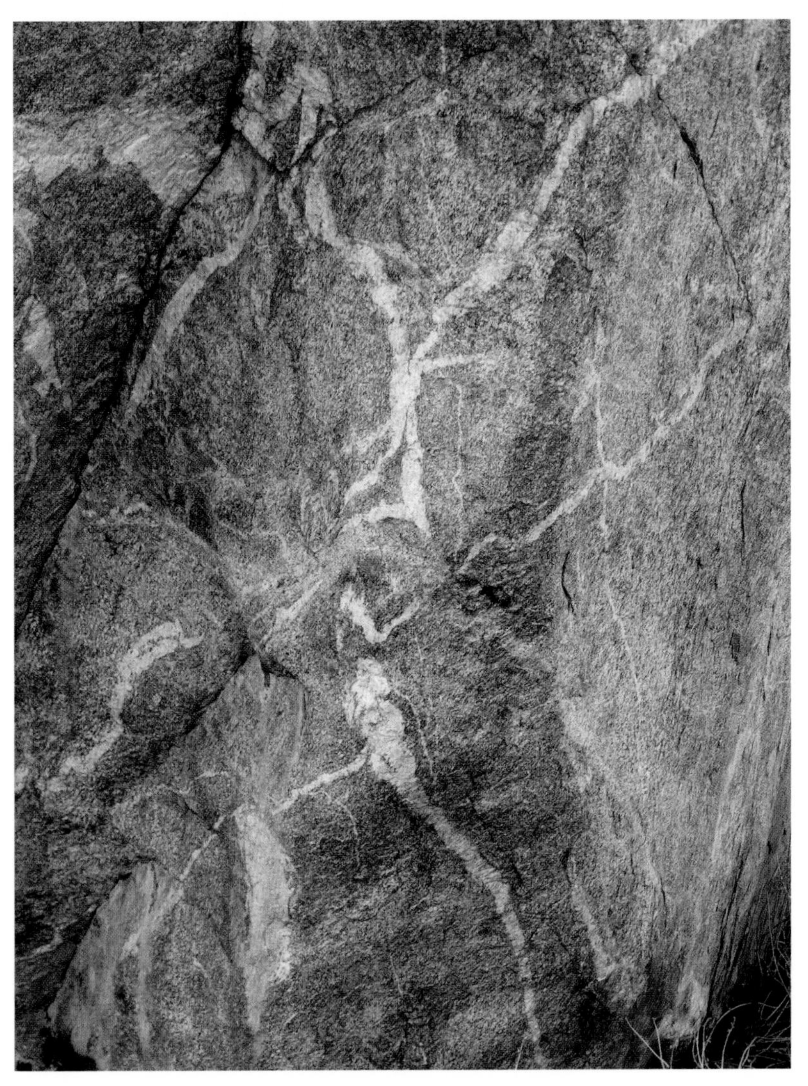

Naturally occurring meander on a sacred rock of the Desert Cahuilla.

Trance perceptions: huge hand and multiple legs. Central Mojave Desert.

A Shaman's Dream Quest

The entopic patterns a shaman perceived could be discrete—or a disorderly swirl. Merging and parting. Rising up, shimmering, overlapping, vanishing. As if from the friction of it all, sparks would fly and sunbursts flare in a riot of psychic turbulence and combustion. And the man's brain yearned for some kind of order—something, anything recognizable—out of this chaos in a dark hollow deep in the earth.

The shaman would cry out for the patterns, the rock, anything to speak to him.

No answer, not yet.

Was he rising or falling? Skimming about or scarcely moving at all?

The shaman would look to his hands and feet. No assurance there. Fingers and toes were twice their normal size, and growing. A tremor crept up his spine to stretch and elongate his body. Didn't he have only two legs and feet, not six or eight? Strange. Perhaps this was a good thing, perhaps there was power in this.

He flew—upward now.

And all around, was his trance state's bizarre miasma beginning to coalesce? To have meaning and power?

Swirling entopic/phosphene patterns.
Little Petroglyph Canyon, western Mojave Desert.

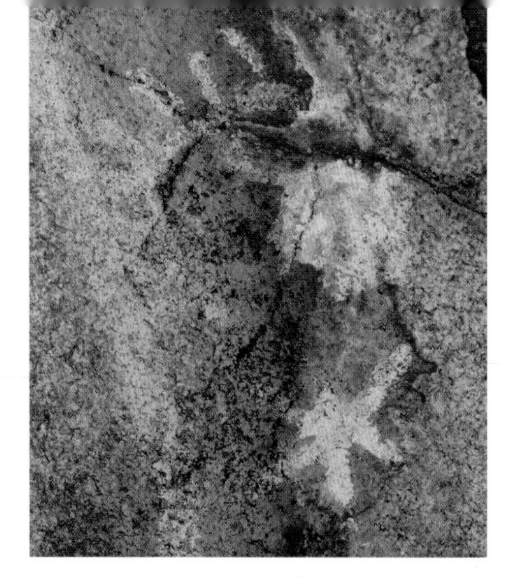

Trances: Transformation

To GAIN OR RENEW POWER, Quechan shamans once followed a pilgrimage trail to Avikwa'ame, their sacred mountain. At its foot, in Grapevine Canyon, there is intriguing evidence of the next stage of a dream quest. (The first was entopic visions; the third and final would be an ecstatic oneness with the supernatural).

Among hundreds of images, stick-figures of shamans appear—not many, just a few. They capture a dream quest perception that hands and feet dispense with digits, and those that remain swell and lengthen. To archaeologists, these figures are "digitate anthromorphs."

These lone figures are surrounded—overwhelmed, actually—by hundreds of images of what the shamans would have visualized. There are phosphenes in abundance, but as well there is a next stage of imagery created as the shaman's mind struggled to make sense of what he was experiencing. Responding to a need for meaning and design, phosphenes would merge—and assume hybrid forms.

Tumbled boulder outcroppings flank the entry to Grapevine Canyon, eastern Mojave Desert. *Left*: A free-falling Kumeyaay shaman.

Note the shaman's crooked elbows and upraised arms, a posture believed to gain power from the sun. The zig-zag likely represents the nearby Colorado River, important in Quechan creation lore.

In his dream quest—as in the opposite petroglyph—the shaman now perceived familiar shapes. Circles radiated power lines, and shone as three suns.[36] An entopic zig-zag became a snake, with a box-like rectangle containing clusters of dots suggesting its eyes. Snakes had a major role in dream quests. Creatures of dread and magic, they had the ability to slither from one world to another, from above ground to below.

Note that below the snake, phosphenes are now packed—corralled, if you will—within the outlines of more-or-less rectangular boxes.

36 Possibly the three suns of creation explored on pp. 8–13.

Detail of Grapevine Canyon's north outcrop.

A New Identity Forms

Across the way in Grapevine Canyon, a red rock wall (next page) features these boxed forms. They were once thought to represent shields, a notion that faded; actual shields were generally circular with little or no adornment. More the case: as shamans psychically refined their visions, they sought and captured a supernatural design—and its inherent, potent power—that would bode them well in the future. It would be, in a sense, a trademark. It would be reproduced on a shaman's ritual shirt.[37]

A closer look at this panel reveals what appears to be a head with a three-feather headdress hovering over the largest of the boxes. It was

37 See pp. 57–61 for an excellent example of this.

Wall of Grapevine Canyon's south outcrop *(above)*; detail *(below)*.

said that a trance could rip a shaman asunder to the extent that all that remained—or so he perceived—was his head. And now that head appeared to be reuniting with a new, magically-generated body.

A shaman morphing—to an otherworldly, symbolic being.

The deepening of a dream quest varied from individual to individual. There was, to be sure, the broad arc of entopics, then transformation, then the supernatural fully realized. In the course of this, there was a disassembly, then a reassembly of a shaman's perceived persona.

At the same time, spirits and ghosts, be they realistic or abstract, crowded about.

As well there was a constantly shifting aural component—whirring, echoing, thundering. Voices could incoherently cry out; or they could quietly, deliberately instruct. Shamans, some claimed, could "see" sounds. Time-wise, all this could come in a rush, or be drawn out over a period of days.

The operative word is *fluidity* in a realm of hyper-vivid trance dreams.

And now, in a final transformational spasm, the shaman and his chosen pattern were merging as one in the same. "The subject stated that he saw fretwork before his eyes, that his arms, hands, and fingers turned into fretwork and that he became identical with fretwork. There was no difference between fretwork and himself."[38] At the same time, vestiges of human form, expression, and identity would dissolve. It had to be terrifying. A man's face would fall away, melt. He would grope for his lips, ears, and nose, and they would rub off. . . . From eyes popped from his head and floating in the air, he would see that his hand was no longer a hand, but a great claw.

"A man ceases to be a man."[39]

38 Heinrich Klüver, *Mescal and Mechanisms of Hallucination*, pp. 71–72.
39 Castaneda, Carlos, *The Teachings of Don Juan: A Yaqui Way of Knowledge*, p. xiii. Reading this, the late Cahuilla shaman Ruby Modesto was to sigh, "We are Don Juans. We are a valley of Don Juans."

Little Petroglyph Canyon, western Mojave Desert.
Next page: Corn Springs, southern Mojave Desert.

Trances: With the Spirits

THE DESERT'S ROCK ART resists interpretation, even as it is increasingly apparent that its images, with little or no exception, are charged with meaning. It helps that many if not most have been demonstrated to be the work of shamans recording their dream quests. In this light, there is a panel in the Mojave Desert bearing the likeness of three shamans, with the legs of the individual to the right grotesquely long and rubbery.

Or might this panel portray a *single* shaman in an ongoing dream quest? The two figures to the left are near identical—with the exception that the first has a filled-in body. Does the difference reflect a symbolic death rendering the shaman a skeletal stick figure? This is questionable, but less so with a look at the figure to the right. Not only are its legs extended—as perceived in a trance state—but the one to the left divides and reforms, and so creates a boxed void. Might this indicate the completion of the transformation in which "a man ceases to be a man"? With an absence, now, of sexual identification.

This is—and forever may be—speculation. That said, it is clear that in the far deserts of the West there were two distinctively different visualizations of a shaman at the height of his dream quest. To the south, he was a stick figure with oversize figures and toes, identified by rock art researchers as a "digitate anthromorph." Further north, a shaman took the form of a "patterned body anthromorph," with a box-like body enclosing an arrangement of entopic symbols.

Whatever his perceived form, a shaman's dream quest would now come to a turning point. His agonies and trials would now be behind him, and his state of mind would verge on—and become—ecstatic.

"Digitate anthromorph." Antelope Hill, central Sonoran Desert.

"Patterned body anthromorph." Grapevine Canyon, eastern Mojave Desert.

Bizarrely transfigured, a shaman and his medicine bag.
Little Petroglyph Canyon, western Mojave Desert.

Spirit Helpers

To comprehend what next occurs, pause for a moment if you will, and revisit the desert world a shaman had taken leave of.

Crossing an alkali dry lake or traversing sun baked badlands, a man or woman might have appeared a lone, lonely figure—but that was an illusion, an illusion dispelled with a footfall's sudden crunch into an underground burrow. And a step further, there could be a plunge into another. All around, the desert floor was pocked with tunnels, ant-size to badger-size. Bugs, reptiles, and mammals by the hundreds, even thousands were down there, still and slumbering.

The desert belonged to its creatures. Man was ephemeral.

Even in the heat of the day, tarantulas wobble onward, males in search of mates. Coyotes prowl. Bighorn sheep forage. Hummingbirds tirelessly seek nectar. Ravens and wrens caw and trill.

Above and below: Western Sonoran Desert.

Come dark, and ever more creatures are abroad. Rustling, hooting, hissing, growling, howling. And their unmistakable presence, echoing in the night air, could well play a role in a shaman's dream quest. Entering and even pursuing a trance state, he'd be aware of activity close by his circle or cave.

It comes as no surprise, then, that a shaman's dreamscape was populated with wildlife. But there was a difference. They could shape-shift.

Above: Western Sonoran Desert.
Below: Little Petroglyph Canyon, western Mojave Desert.

These animals could first appear as a light or pattern, then as a human, and finally—as they came to trust a shaman—as themselves.

These animals could talk, often in staccato bursts.

They could become a shaman's spirit helper.

Animals, it was believed, were once the first Indians—the first beings created—and possessed far greater power than any man now. Regardless of their size, no matter that they were harmless or dangerous.

A kaleidoscope of creatures could aid a shaman. Fly, ant, bee, cricket, lizard, quail, crow, fox, badger, bighorn sheep, mountain lion, even the occasional bear that had strayed into the desert. Centipedes were unusually powerful.

A shaman would be wary of mountain lions and bears; they could be dangerously powerful.

But, according to Paiute shaman Joe Green, "Shamans never got power from Coyote. According to the old stories the Indians tell, Coyote always spoils everything. Coyote is bad. Sometimes he tries to get the soul of someone. He says, 'I am going to get you when you die. I will eat you'."[40]

And Frog? Only evil shamans—sorcerers—had business with frogs.

Once a spirit helper announced itself, it was important that it be obeyed and never doubted. A shaman's relative might be deathly ill, only to have his animal spirit helper caution him not to attempt a cure on the grounds that he was insufficiently prepared.

Properly treated, though, spirit helpers offered a range of powers efficacious in curing a range of serious illnesses. As well they could assure a good harvest, charm a hunter's game, control the weather, even steady the hand of a gambler. Accordingly, a shaman would seek out—and rely on—ever more creatures. Ethnographer Willard Z. Park canvassed latter-day Paiute shamans as to the sources of their power. Rosie Plummer was content with a rattlesnake; Mary Garvey conversed with a crow and a big mountain fly; George Calico relied on a lizard and two water babies dwelling in a nearby lake. At the same lake, Abraham Mahwee had settled on "a large spotted bird, and the ghost of three Indians, the kind of people who live far away where nobody can see them."[41] Spirit helpers, incidentally, weren't exclusively animals. Ghosts, clouds, the moon and sun—all could bestow power.

40 Quoted in Willard Z. Park, *Shamanism in Western North America*, p.19.
41 *Ibid*, p. 18.

A shaman absorbs the power of the sun. Little Petroglyph Canyon, western Mojave Desert.

These Paiute shamans were restrained in their needs. Others sought a half dozen, even a dozen or more spirit helpers in the course of repeated dream quests.

Spirit helpers not only bestowed power, but schooled shamans in its proper use. They described in detail each step of a ritual, and taught songs to accompany those steps. So it was that every shaman had songs that were his and his alone. They weren't long songs, but rather short phrases, to be hypnotically repeated over and over again, often punctuated—and dramatized—with unintelligible syllables. In effect: a verbal form of drumming. A northern Paiute example:

Pagu'nava'! Pagu'nava'!
Tungwu'kwiji! Tungwu'kwiji!
Wumbe'doma'! Wumbe'doma'!

Fog! Fog!
Lightning! Lightning!
Whirlwind! Whirlwind![42]

In a Dream World: Ceremonies and Dances

Guided by a spirit helper, a shaman would witness spectral ceremonies, and become proficient in the dances he would perform and lead. This could well have inspired a pictograph of two "Happy Ipays" (named after a Kumeyaay clan). Their stick-figure form and over-size hands and toes signal a trance state; their body language evokes elation, even ecstasy.

42 Cited in Michael Hittman, *Wovoka and the Ghost Dance*, p. 300.

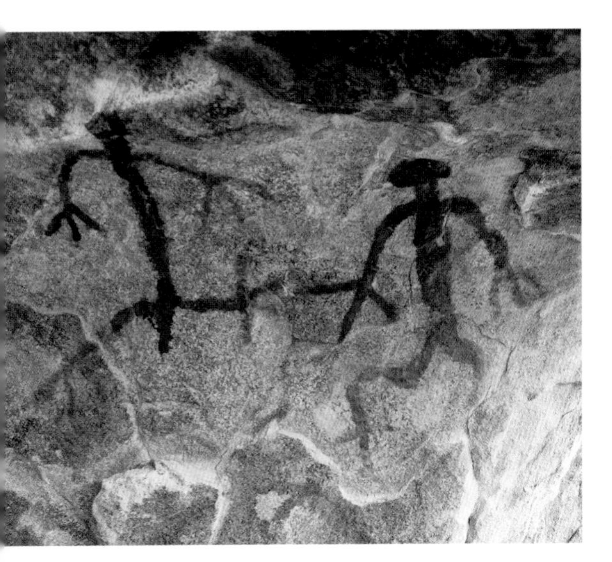

A change of angle animates a "happy Ipay" dance. Western Sonoran Desert.

In the company of his spirit helper, the shaman would now further explore the dreamscape of his mind. Apparitions would materialize and vanish. And, as evidence that all was surreal and fluid, the shaman and his creature would bond—and merge, *the two become one*. As an illustration of this, there's a boulder at McCoy Springs in the southern Mojave.

Part snake, part man.

How better to acquire a spirit helper's power? And here, the shaman didn't let it go at that. A quail topknot would make him a hybrid human-snake-bird. There was considerable magic in this: a synthesis creating an impossible being that could both burrow in the earth or fly in the sky—and either way, access the supernatural.

However long a shaman's trance state may have lasted in real time—possibly days—it was taken to last a single night, or in the spirit world, a bright paradisiacal day (in the belief that time and landscape in the supernatural was the opposite of that in the natural). So, as darkness enveloped a dream world, the sun rose in an everyday world.

Come Morning: Remembering and Capturing

In the cave beyond the Funeral Mountains where our consideration of a dream quest began three chapters ago, its shaman would have stirred and—however exhausted or even if in pain—set to work.

As with all dreams, details of his quest would quickly fade, even vanish, unless he committed them to rock that very morning. He would have pigments on hand, often charcoal for black, natural chalk or kaolin clay for white, and hematite or iron oxide for red. That would be his palette. A chewed twig or his finger would suffice as a brush.

As the rock art in the cave likely reflects multiple dream quests, it's impossible to sort out what the shaman would have recorded at the completion of any given trance. But, looking about, there are suggestions of what, in sum, transpired.

Here again is the cave's major, south wall panel.

To the far left: an undistorted red figure *not* in a trance state. Close by, concentric circles suggest a portal into a dream world. As well, there is a series of ten black tick marks. Numerous explanations have been offered for these, with the consensus that they're counting something. Possibilities: the number of dream quests pursued at the site, how many spirit helpers were accumulated in the course of those quests, or how many songs a shaman learned. (And the meaning of such marks could vary from shaman to shaman.)

To the far right: An ethereal shaman with his hand grasping the head of a lizard spirit helper.

In the center: An ovoid figure, partially faded by exfoliation or water damage beneath a horizontal crack. Whatever this represents, it is important, for it is positioned between a shaman's mundane and mystical worlds. Now this is speculation, but what we have here could be a bizarre mask of death suggestive of the dying and rebirth a shaman experienced at the onset of his trance state. In the American Southwest, death is traditionally a square or round-faced disembodied head.[43]

43 See examples, p. 78.

Northern Mojave panel (reprised from page 89).

As to what the shaman experienced in his trance state, a panel on the cave's western wall offers a possibility: two rows of diminutive figures, and among them, a bighorn sheep and possibly a deer.

Humans and spirits joined in a dance?

So it was that throughout the desert, aspects of dream quests were pecked and daubed upon hundreds of rock panels. Though it is doubtful that they will ever be fully decoded, they are testimony to thousands of dream journeys, and the power they offered a shaman in a harsh and uncertain life and world.

There is a telling image at the southern edge of that world, at a Kumeyaay site near the Mexican border. A shaman grasps a spirit helper, possibly newly acquired. Five more are ranged at his feet. With the exception of an unmistakable bird, their identity is uncertain (Two bees? A red ant? A centipede—or a snake?)

The shaman had reason to be pleased with himself. He has braved a realm where "a man ceases to be a man" and, with a half-dozen spirits now at his call, he could rejoin his people as "a man of power."

Western Sonoran Desert

Journey to the Land of Fire

In a shaman's mind, the intensity—startling and wrenching—of what he had encountered in his realm of the spirits would fade, but its revelations—preserved in rock art—would remain. From his dream quest cave or circle, he would return to his village and the company of his clan. The walk could take a few minutes or several days.

Deep in his psyche, the shaman would have braved the unknown and gained the power of efficacious dream animals. Yet outwardly, there would be little to set him apart. He would laugh, joke, feast, and gamble. He would hunt (though not the species of a helper). He would take a wife, and they'd have children. He would often be his clan's headman. Only when called to cure or lead a ceremony would he don his animal skin and feather costume, and with it the mantle of a man possessed, a man who on his hands and knees could howl as a wild animal. Onlookers wouldn't see, but nevertheless would *know* that the shaman had become one with a spirit helper, and could draw on its power.

Dawn, Tomesha. Northern Mojave Desert.

Most often, shamans were lone practitioners. But on occasion they might call in other shamans to help with difficult cures. There are Cahuilla accounts of shamans being a clubby lot, even when nothing was up. There is further record of Chemehuevi and Paiute shamans sojourning among the Cahuilla, evidence that shamans—as many western Indians—were given to roaming. In the desert, a tribe would attend another's festivals. Similarly, a shaman might travel dozens or hundreds of miles to acquire specific skills.

Like curing snakebites.

A Cahuilla could call on a neighboring Kumeyaay adept at this. In exchange, the Cahuilla could have offered a concoction of wild tobacco and elephant tree bark that, ingested, could grant power to a hunting shaman.

In her *Autobiography*, Kumeyaay Delfina Cuero recalls:

> Snakes are kind of mean and you have to keep your eyes open all the time. My great uncle—a snake man—claimed the snakes would come and talk to him and tell him when they were going to bite someone. Then he could already be on his way to the

person. When halfway there, he hollered three times, and the person dying could hear him.

My great uncle danced around him, and he got well.[44]

There was more to this. A slow chant would quiet the patient, as would his body stroked with a feather. Indeed, this could effectively slow the spread of venom and prevent a fatal amount from reaching and stopping the heart. Even so, once recovered, a victim was toxic. Recalled Delfino, "If a person who has been bitten goes into my garden, all the plants will die, or else produce no fruit, or just dry up."

A Shaman's Desert Odyssey

A network of trails linked the desert's tribes. Carefully tended, they were a uniform four hand spans wide, cleared of pebbles, and marked by cairns, arrows, and petroglyphs. It was important to stick to these trails; straying risked the mischief of malign spirits.

With a steady, unrelenting jog, an Indian messenger could cover an astounding hundred miles a day. A party of traders—or a shaman—would log perhaps a quarter of that, yet enough to accomplish journeys of several hundred miles in a matter of weeks.

It has been theorized that some four thousand years ago the tribes of the far western deserts were chronically belligerent. At each others' throats, raiding, pillaging. But then there was a realization that to survive in an increasingly harsh environment (following the last Ice Age), they needed to put aside their clubs and atlatls, and cooperate in sharing scarce resources. The spirit of this endured, and a roaming individual could expect warm welcomes, hospitality, and the sharing of lore and knowledge.

44 This and the following quote from Florence C. Shipek, *Delfina Cuero: Her Autobiography*, p. 47 and pp, 48–9

Moreover, the very act of wandering was an end—an opportunity to experience the desert's shifting moods and unexpected marvels. To appreciate and absorb its beauty. There was magic in a scorched, dun brown landscape mystically transformed by swirling clouds and glowing light.

To the Land of the Quechan

So it was that a footloose Cahuilla shaman might readily journey from a Laguna Mountain village of a Kumeyaay snake man to the banks of the Colorado River, the home of renowned Quechan fracture and stun shamans. They could skillfully set bones; they could right disoriented souls.

The Cahuilla shaman's odyssey might then have swung north along the Colorado River to the sacred peak of Awikwa'ame. This "Spirit" or

Cahuilla trail and cairn. Western Sonoran Desert.

Above: Picacho Peak, sacred to the Quechan.
Below: Clearing sandstorm, land of the Quechan.

"Dead" mountain was key to the dream quests of Quechan shamans. Rather than actively initiate a trance and plunge into the realm of the supernatural—the case with the Cahuilla and most other desert tribes—the Quechan passively, patiently awaited dreams that connected them to the time and power of their creator-god Kumastamxo. A Quechan shaman was to recall, "When a little boy I took a trip to Avikwa'ame Mountain

Above: Panamint Valley, Shoshone-Coso land.
Below: Toquima Range, land of the Shoshone.

and slept at its base." He dreamt of climbing higher. "At last I reached the willow-roof in front of the Dark House there. Kumastamxo was within. It was so dark that I could hardly see him. He was naked and very large. Only a few great doctors were in there with him."[45]

45 Quoted in A. L. Kroeber, *Handbook of the Indians of California*, p. 784.

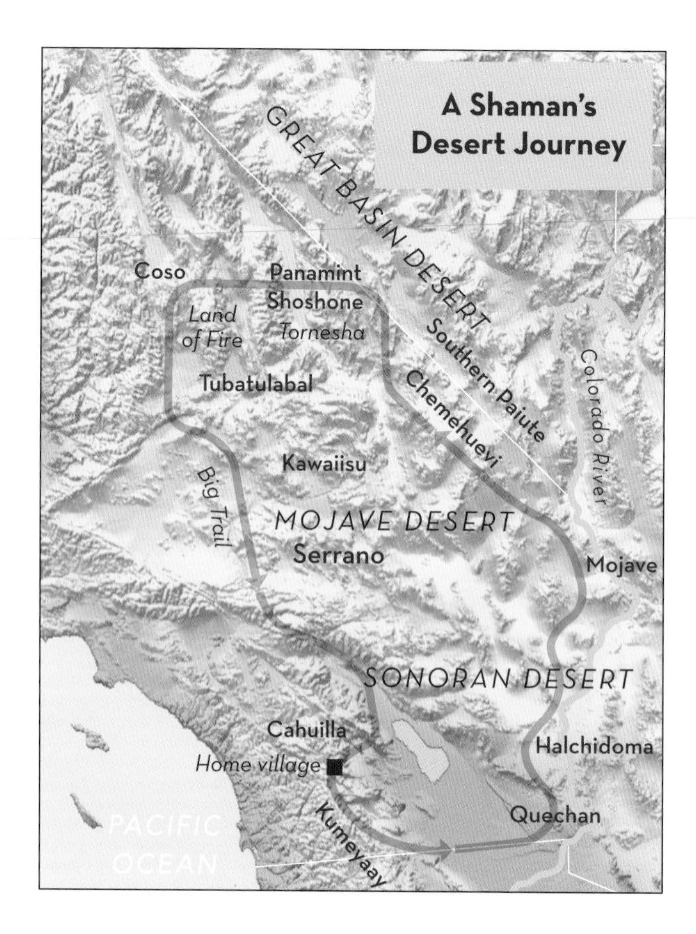

As the Cahuilla had schemed to kill and then cremate their creator-god Mukat, the Quechan had stopped short of that. Kumastamxo, instead, had been relegated to a shadowy half-life.

Despite the difference, the lives of the shamans of the two tribes was much the same. Along the river, there was knowledge to be shared: of cures, songs, and perhaps a sly illusion or two.

And there was a constant: in the eyes of both tribes, earthly power had become the province of shamans.

Not their creator-gods.

The Mojaves

On up the Colorado River, the Mojaves were a tough lot. Entering their territory, an itinerant Cahuilla shaman would have watched his step. Widely feared, the Mojaves took exception to the notion of peace in the desert. They supported a disciplined warrior class—the *Kwanamis*—that, armed with "potato masher" clubs, took gratuitous delight in raiding the villages of neighboring tribes. In parties ranging from ten to twelve stealthy individuals, they had surprise on their side; even so, facing considerable odds they were often the worse for wear. Accordingly, there was a need for arrow shamans who, as well as singing a cure, had a talent for physically extracting arrowheads, and staunching, salving, and binding wounds.

With the coming of the whites and their weapons, arrow shamans expanded their practice.

They became gunshot shamans.

The Chemehuevi

Further north, our shaman could have fallen in with a band of Chemehuevi, traders in salt and medicinal herbs. They would travel the West for months at a time, from Utah to the Pacific Ocean. "They delighted to visit strange peoples, speak strange tongues, sing strange songs, and marry strange wives."[46] Yet for all they saw and experienced, they passionately believed their land by the Colorado River were the best on earth, all a man could ask for.

46 John P. Harrington, *The Chemehuevis: Their Name, Character, and Habitat*, p. 4.

Of interest to a curious Cahuilla: A Chemehuevi shaman had no use for a feathered headdress, ritual shirt or skirt, or regalia of any kind. Instead, he placed his trust in his *poro,* a wand in the shape of a shepherd's crook. It was his badge of office, and a power unto itself. It could stand up and talk, though only a shaman could hear it. Its touch, its rap, could magically heal.

On a lighter note, our Cahuilla shaman might have been amused by a preponderance of shamans named for their physical quirks. Head-bent-back, One-eye, Walking-stick-man, Crooked-feet, and Big-ass (a sorcerer).

Known for their "elfin expression, which is sufficient certificate of their rascality," the Chemehuevi had a "gleeful consciousness . . . which keeps them in an excellent humor."[47] On the trail they were inveterate gamblers fond of *peon,* a guessing game requiring a quick mind and agile hand and body movements. A Cahuilla shaman could well have joined in, even had an edge with the aid of a gaming-inclined spirit helper.

The Chemehuevi were good company.

On to the Lands of the Paiute and the Shoshone

However he wandered, whatever route a shaman took, he would be drawn to *Tomesha,* in the language of the Shoshone, "ground afire." Several desert tribes shared a belief that this was the forge of creation, an ancestral *tiwiingarivipi,* "sacred land, mythic country."

Even though Tomesha—today's Death and Panamint valleys—has for centuries been the hottest place on earth, there is abundant evidence of a long sequence of occupation. Elaborate and puzzling, ancient rock alignments and patterns wend across low-lying mesas.

47 Lt. Joseph C. Ives, *Report upon the Colorado River of the West,* p. 55–56.

Nearing Tomesha, a beckoning glow.

Hundreds of petroglyphs and pictographs are tucked in shadowy niches and crawl up near-vertical walls.

A shaman passing through could not help but appreciate Tomesha's sweep and wonder. At dawn and dusk, a vast landscape was transformed, and glowed in shades of purple, bluish-brown, almond, and rose. Even in the blazing white heat of midday, mirages conjured shimmering lakes and inviting groves of palms. In spring, yellow and white flowers cloaked hills and mountains as far as the eye could see.

Our shaman would at once be awestruck and anxious. Trudging across blazing salt flats, there was a song for this:

It is not difficult to imagine Tomesha as a primordial land where a creator-god fashioned and "stood up" a first people.

At Fire Valley
Cut off by fire, cut off by fire.
At Fire Valley,
Cut off by fire, cut off by fire.[48]

Here, springs were few and far between, and could be easily fouled by wild animals or run dry. No water, and death would tread a man's footfalls. It would be a relief for a shaman to clear Tomesha, and continue his odyssey.

On to the Coso Mountains

To the west of Tomesha lay the slate blue Cosos, with "Coso" a word for "fire" among the indigenous Kawaaiisu and Coso Indians. Despite the blazing imagery, the Cosos offered a welcome change from open desert and alkali dry lakes rippling with heat waves. As a shaman climbed higher and higher, oddly-gesticulating, towering Joshua trees filled the landscape, a shift from scrub mesquite struggling for survival. The air was temperate. Clear cold springs abounded, and as well as healing hot springs. It could rain, even snow; a single deep valley separated the Cosos from the white-capped Sierra Nevadas.

Throughout the Cosos, reddish-black cinder cones erupted from the landscape, and our shaman would have kept to trails skirting crinkled rivers of basalt—lava frozen in time—as they flowed across upland mesas. Indeed, volcanic activity could be the point of a Coso petroglyph that at first glance appears a collage of entopic patterns, but may in fact be the record of an eruption as recent as six hundred years ago.

48 Quoted in Carobeth Laird, *Mirror and Pattern*, p. 293.

Volcano peak of the Coso Mountains.
Western Mojave Desert.

Joshua trees thrive at higher elevations.

The possible record of a volcanic eruption—with flames spouting from a crater, a sinuous lava flow, and a figure (to the left) who could have lost his life in the event. Above, the hand of a second, shaman-like figure reaches out, possibly to quell the mayhem.

Soon a roaming shaman would find himself on the brink of one or another flood-cut canyons. Narrow and shallow at first, but then deepening in their course. Scrambling down, he would encounter a sole petroglyph, then another, and finally he'd be overwhelmed by hundreds of them. Some thirty miles of Coso canyons are engraved with nearly 15,000 rock art images, the largest concentration in the New World.

Here was the handiwork of shamans over the last ten millennia, with Little Petroglyph Canyon a major haunt.

The north wall of Little Petroglyph Canyon. Western Mojave Desert.

Here, rain shamans pursued their dream quests.

Depending on the season, the year, or even the century, a few shamans—or dozens—would have taken up residence in the canyon's sandy bottom or in niches and shelves indented in its walls. In a desert afternoon, they would doze, drum, and if they were inclined, prepare hallucinogenic drugs in anticipation of a night's dream quest.

The Puzzle of the Coso Bighorn Sheep

All about, pecked images of bighorn sheep, by the hundreds, scampered across the canyon's walls and rocks. They far outnumbered a scattering of rock art snakes and lizards and the odd centipede and spider.[49]

The question to pioneering archaeologists, ethnographers, and even curious Indians was: Why?

49 Throughout the Cosos, researchers have tallied over 7,600 images of sheep, measuring from a few inches to four feet across.

Up until the late 1960s, the consensus was: hunting magic. By replicating the bighorns, a people could control them, charm them, then kill them as favored game. This was bolstered by a number of images of sheep shot with bows and arrows.

But then, in the early 1970s, a UCLA team directed by David Whitley spent four years excavating a village site at the western edge of the Cosos. Petroglyphs abounded, and middens were layered with an assortment of faunal remains:

> Thousands of rabbit bones, dozens of pack-rat bones, a few deer bones, and an occasional bird or reptile bone. There was only one mountain sheep bone, representing less that one-tenth of one percent of animal remains from the site. Other sites in the area produced similar results.[50]

50 James L. Pierson, *Shamanism and the Ancient Mind,* p 147.

In Little Petroglyph Canyon.

A herd of phantom sheep—and falling rain.

Apparently, not a single bighorn had been brought down by spear or arrow. A hunting magic explanation may have been valid for other cultures and sites, but clearly not here.

David Whitley and others now scratched their heads and advanced a new theory to explained the Cosos' herds of petroglyph sheep. Their answer was a metaphor etched in stone: *Sheep were equated with rain*. And indeed, the link is made in a number of Little Petroglyph Canyon images.

Though perhaps baffling to us, this metaphor would have struck our Cahuilla shaman as a natural association. His environment, though hundreds of miles distant, had much in common with the Cosos when it came to weather. Coastal storms would move inland over mountains (the Lagunas to the south, the Sierra Nevadas to the north), to then be stalled by updrafts welling from the desert. The stalemate creates a "rain shadow." Clouds hovered on the horizon, with the shadow of rain—only the shadow—cast to the arid lands to the east.

Consider in this light, a cause-and-effect sequence of events.

1. At the crest of barrier mountains, clouds would roil for days at a time—to every so often break free and sweep over the desert.

2. Rain would fall. In as little as three days, lowland desert trees and shrubs would leaf out.

3. In hot, dry times, bighorns favor remote, higher elevations,
but now would be drawn by the prospect of fresh grazing.
4. Additional often violent storms would trigger flash floods.
Flowers would bloom. The desert would be transformed.

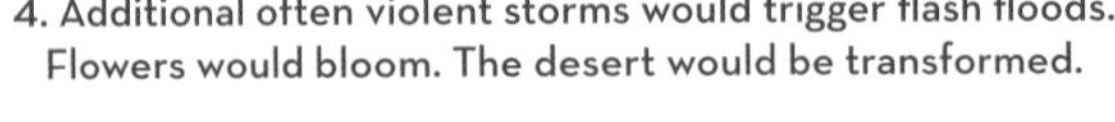

5. Bighorns would now spend weeks, even months at lower elevations—and be far more apparent to the land's Indians.

When rain falls, sheep appear.

The two were intertwined. So it was that if a shaman sought bighorns as his spirit helpers—and so assumed their identity—then he, like they, could control the weather.[51]

So far, so good, but what of Coso images of men killing sheep, or of sheep slain by throwing sticks or arrows? If this wasn't magic to assure luck in a hunt, what was it?

UCLA's David Whitley and others have offered a rationale for this.

Given the metaphor in which *sheep were equated with rain*, the petroglyphs in question could depict shamans dominating the weather, for by magically killing a bighorn they could invoke the creature's power. This is supported by an Indian comment recorded some eighty years ago: "*It is*

51 It was apparently of little or no concern that in reality the weather materialized the sheep, not the sheep the weather.

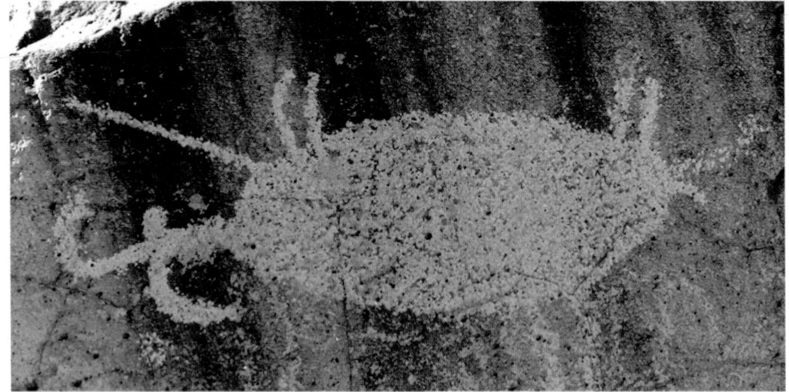

The bighorn's downturned tail is a sign of death.

To the upper right, note the figure with the spear or
bow—rounding out a sheep-rain-killing association.

said that rain falls when a mountain sheep is killed. Because of this some mountain sheep dreamers thought they were rain doctors." [52]

The metaphor becomes more complex with the possibility that these images could *also* represent the first stage of a dream quest in which a shaman "dies," only to be reborn—with, in this case, the shaman one in the same as the spirit helper he slays. In effect, he would be shooting himself, offering himself as a sacrifice to initiate his dream quest.

The Dream Quests of Rain Shamans

Come night in the Cosos, Little Petroglyph and other canyons would echo with the drumming and chanting of shamans drawn from as far away as the Gulf of California and the Uinta Mountains of northeastern Utah. Their trance techniques would have varied. Some would have fasted or were sleep-deprived, others would have ingested datura or wild tobacco.

In the mists of visions soon to possess them, bighorn sheep would materialize—clattering across rocky slopes, guardians of their high desert realm—and offer themselves as spirit helpers.

Guided by their bighorns, shamans would learn rituals to summon the wind, order rain to fall, or have the rays of the sun pierce and scatter dark clouds.

As a shaman's world was a secretive world, little is known of how this was practiced. There exists, though, the life and magic of one Bob Rabbit, the last known rain shaman of the Kawaiisu. Though characterized as a "poor, erratic informant," Bob Rabbit nevertheless offered lively, if sketchy recitals of pilgrimages to the Cosos, where he joined other shamans "in painting his face with the red clay of the hot springs so that he might be recognized by magic spirals of the wind, or a whirlwind."

52 Isabel T. Kelly, "Chemehuevi Shamanism," p. 139.

As a young man,

> Bob said he had acquired his [rain-making] songs in dreams after he had eaten tobacco lime. He further revealed details of a rain-making kit featuring a steatite bowl carefully lined with moist mud and embedded with pinyon nuts, chia seeds, and acorns. He would cover the mixture with the skin of a fawn, and then smoke his pipe three times, three being his ritual number. Next he would raise a bone tube to his lips and through it blow one, then two, then three times, and so raise the wind."[53]

Bob's account of what followed was vague. He would draw a circle in the sand, then add a line pointing north and south. He would produce crystals from his medicine bag, though what exactly he did with them he didn't say. He prided his finesse, claiming that he could simultaneously invoke rain and cold weather, "but it did not blow or freeze, and there was a good stand of filaree."

To banish a storm: "Bob chewed weeds and water. He spat into the fire, steam rises, and the rain stops in three days from that time."

Come Morning in the Cosos

With the first glimmer of dawn, the canyon's resident and visiting shamans would have looked to their hands and feet and seen them to be as they always had been—except in a previous night's bizarre dream state. So that the power granted in that state not be forfeit, Little Petroglyph Canyon would have reverberated with rocks hammering quartz crystals. It was imperative that shamans commit their bizarre dream selves to

53 The source for this account is David Whitley et. al., *The Archaeology of Ayers Rock*, p. 44 and pp. 47–8.

desert-varnished, blackened rock—the rock itself charged with power and magic.

A mile-long stretch of the canyon is a testament to this—a bizarre, mystic gallery, unrivaled not only in the deserts of the far West, but in all of North America.

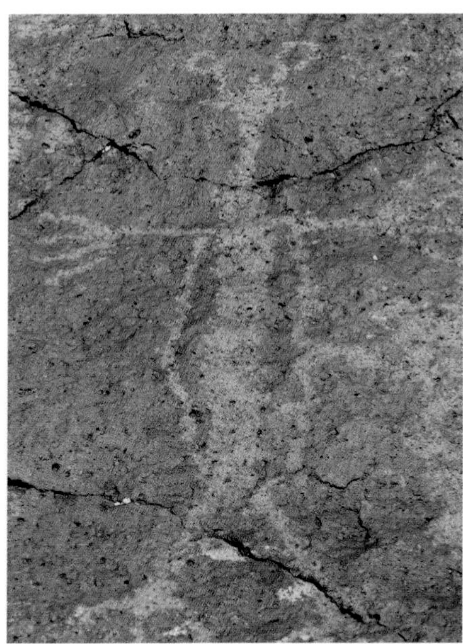

At a turn in the canyon, a grand gathering of shamans.

In the glare of the midday sun, the intensity of a shaman's vision would diminish, its outline and details blurring and fading. But by then, he would have recorded an image of his supernatural self.

There is no knowing how many dream quests it would have taken—only one, a dozen, more?—for an individual to learn the arcane rites and songs that would confirm his role as a weather shaman. In good time, the day would come when he would pack his medicine bag, and take his leave of fellow shamans drawn to the Cosos from the length and breadth of the desert West.

Now, he would head south along the "Big Trail." Skirting the foothills of the Sierras and wending from spring to spring, it offered an easy route home.

For a roaming Cahuilla shaman and others, the journey was about power, and back in his home village, an ability to control the weather in times of drought or flood. And, as he chose, he might casually demonstrate—boast, if you will—his sway over the supernatural. With the wave of a feather or a magical song, he would conjure clouds in a clear sky; at his bidding, the wind would rise or suddenly be stilled.

Cahuilla Ruby Modesto was in awe of this power, offhandedly demonstrated by her grandfather Francisco:

> He used to call the wind when it was hot. He whistled two long notes. And it never failed. The wind came along. "Oh how wonderful," he'd say, "a nice wind to cool your body."
>
> He had the power all right! [54]

54 Ruby Modesto and Guy Mount, *Not for Innocent Ears*, p. 36.

Whirlswinds were believed to harbor shamans in magical flight.

Pursuit of a Lost Soul

DESERT TRIBESMEN, women, and children were wary of the approach of a whirlwind, for it might not only blister and blind with sand crystals, but harbor ghosts of the dead. Restless ghosts, on the prowl for company. Indians would cast dirt in is direction, shouting, "Stay away from me! You are no good. I can see you. I know what you are. You go the other way!"[55]

A shaman, though, might welcome—even invoke—a whirlwind. He saw himself immune to the mischief of ghosts. Moreover, they could impart knowledge of the land of the dead, and how, in magical flight, to venture there. It is not that a shaman wanted to do this, but sometimes he had to when a man or woman's soul strayed from its body, and had to be pursued and recovered.

Cahuilla Ruby Modesto recounts the story of a man whose soul took to wandering, and though it always returned, he was sufficiently

55 Willard Z. Park, *Shamanism in Western North America*, p. 40.

alarmed to seek out her Uncle Charlie, a shaman schooled by ghosts in soul recovery.

> He was simply falling asleep all the time. He couldn't work, do anything. It was causing a lot of trouble in his life. Two of Uncle Charlie's apprentices were there, and I was there too. Uncle Charlie was in charge. His apprentices sang and danced. The sick man sat watching the fire. Suddenly he fell asleep. Uncle Charlie and the puls ran outside. They said the Soul had left the man's body and was trying to escape.
>
> Uncle Charlie followed it to our graveyard, just down the road, where the sick man's relatives were buried. Uncle Charlie said that the Soul wanted to dig itself into the ground. It was trying to go down into the grave. Uncle Charlie said it was probably disgusted with the way that the man was living his life. The Soul just wanted to die. But Uncle Charlie stomped the ground above the grave. He stamped it hard with his boots and the Soul couldn't get back into the earth. Then Uncle Charlie caught it. He blew tobacco smoke on the Soul and put it back through the top portion of the head from which the Soul emerges. Then he brushed the man's head with eagle feathers. After that the man was OK. He woke up and stopped having so much trouble in his life.[56]

As doctoring went, this was a relatively easy case.

For critical cases, there would be signs—omens—of a strayed soul. A bird or animal would behave strangely; a star would fall from the sky.

A shaman would don his ceremonial shirt and headdress, gather up his kit, and await his call—or even be on his way to a victim's dwelling, guided by a spirit helper.

56 Ruby Modesto and Guy Mount, *Not for Innocent Ears*, p. 45.

Paiute shaman Bull Tom

A race would be on, for the signs a shaman would have seen would have also alerted soul-snatching spirits. To the Cahuilla these numbered Hulim, Tukaiel, Temaiaukel, Tevlevel, and the supremely evil shaman-gone-bad Tahquitz.

Who would claim the errant soul?

Often, a soul has taken flight for several hours, even days—cause for not only a shaman to be called, but a shaman of sufficient power. As reported by Paiute Joe Green, his friend Captain Dave had all but died. Two shamans had struggled to save him, only to give up. "His mind was gone." But then, shaman Bull Tom was on the scene.

Means of magical flight: a whirlwind and flying as a bird.

Bull Tom declared:

> "I am going to lie down here. I am going to find him. His mind is already gone. Maybe I cannot find him. I do not know how long he has been gone. Maybe it is too long." Bull Tom was in a trance for a long time. Then he was heard talking softly. He was still a long way off. We heard him say, "Do not be afraid. We are going home. We are going back to your home. We will go from here over to that mountain. Your boy, your daughter, our wife are all there. We are going back and see all of them. Do not look back. Bad animals are back there. Do not go back; we will be home soon."
>
> Then Bull Tom came out of his trance. He told Captain Dave's family to blow on the top of Captain Dave's head. Captain Dave woke up. He recognized all the people around him. He recovered and lived for many years. [57]

57 Willard Z. Park, *Shamanism in Western North America*, p. 59.

That is what observers Joe Green and others saw and heard. As for Bull Tom: In a trance state, he had undertaken a perilous and possibly fatal journey. If anyone or anything—say, the howl of a coyote—awakened him, he could well have died, for, pursuing Captain Dave, his soul as well had left its body.

Outside of Captain Dave's dwelling, a whirlwind might have gathered and spun to the sky—or a strange bird had winged to the stars and beyond: Bull Tom, transformed in magical flight.

Bull Tom's soul was on its way to the land of the dead. By now, that's where Captain Dave's soul would likely be found, if found at all.

Other than agreeing on its hazards, desert tribes vary in their descriptions of a pursuing shaman's journey. To the Quechan, a soul, ascending from the earth, passed through a windless haze of dust, then was enveloped by an eerie white fog.

For the Cahuilla, twin crags then loomed. Flanking the entrance to the land of the dead, they were engaged in ceaseless, eternal motion. They would crash together, then separate. A guardian spirit—*Montakwet*—would challenge a shaman flown from earth. Could he create a figure with string threaded through his fingers? Another? And another, until Montakwet was satisfied and the shaman was free to pass through the teetering crags, but only if he respected his elders and had lived a good, generous life. If not, he'd be crushed, and his soul recast as a bat or rock in the shadow of the crags.

If nimbly surviving the hazard, the shaman would travel a road to the east, formed by a whisker of the god Mukat. Further perils would ensue. He could drown crossing a raging river. On an impossibly steep trail, he could lose his footing, and fall suddenly and hopelessly back to earth.

To the contrary, the whisker road's journey could be pleasantly, if eerily, serene. Everything would be quite the opposite of what it was in the shaman's desert home. Night would be day. Gentle, cool breezes would blow. Leafy trees would offer their shade. Rivers flowed and lakes abounded. Encountering souls of the dead, the shaman could hear their

Atlatl Rock, eastern Mojave Desert.

bones rattling, but saw them to be quite enjoying themselves, blessed with foods bitter on earth, but now tasty, exceptionally so.

But a shaman was not to be lulled. Without warning, a bloodthirsty monster could rear up, attack, and devour him.

There is no written or verbal account of exactly how a desert shaman would seek out a fugitive soul. There are, though, petroglyphs that may well describe this—as on a panel high on a red rock outcrop in Nevada's Valley of Fire State Park.

Shaking off his trance, a shaman psychically returned to his desert home would look to his patient, and with relief, see him back in the land of the living, free of dead relatives who in their paradisiacal land had murmured, "Stay, join us." Typically, the shaman would thereupon

From a shaman's footprint, a line—a route, a path?—ascends a precipitous slope.

Detail: A bighorn bleeding from the mouth suggests a shaman's near-death as he became one with a spirit helper—and gained the animal's magical power.

Detail of preceding panel:
Oasis palms—symbolic of a lush, verdant land of the dead?

This is speculative, but the two uppermost figures could represent the soul of a shaman and an errant soul he's sought, located, and would now coax from the land of the dead and guide back to his home and family. With the warning: "Do not look back . . ."

regale family and friends with an account of his journey and rescue, and its perils. Braving icy winds and burning forests. Crossing bloody streams. But these perils counted for naught, for the shaman's power, swelling with each new challenge, had proved unassailable.

Awed, the crowd would be murmur their appreciation and gratitude.

In a shaman's world, power was all. "It was held to be the soul and summary of existence. . . . It was the mind of the universe."[58]

And power could precipitate a shaman's downfall, his death. Just suppose a shaman returned to earth from his magical flight, unsteadily rose to his feet, and saw that his patient had died. Relatives gathered about the body, crying and wailing, would turn on him in hot-eyed anger. If he was so blessed with power, why had this happened? The only answer was that he was up to no good. Power being amoral, he had malignly bewitched his patient!

An Owens Valley Tragedy

A shaman was generally allowed three successive failures—before he would be set upon and "quietly murdered." In the face of this, some fled, some admitted to sorcery and repented, and in the year 1876, shaman after shaman lost their lives in the Owens Valley to the north of the Coso Mountains.

This is what happened. White settlers had usurped Paiute lands. For farming, to run cattle. They had dispersed the inhabitants of age-old villages, driven them to a marginal existence in the hills and mountains flanking the valley. They as well cursed the Paiute with measles, an Old World disease alien to a native American natural resistance. A few cases mushroomed to an epidemic, with shamans called to frantically chant, suck, and hopelessly fail in their ministrations.

58 Jay Miller, *Shamanic Odyssey*, p. 151

In a rare 1888 panorama taken by writer Mary Austin, a surviving Owens Valley shaman performs a "medicine dance" before assembled Paiutes, with curious whites looking on.

These doctors would fail a first time, then another, and then a third. As reported in an Owens Valley newspaper:

> The destruction of doctors and their families has been frightful. In the upper end of the valley, eighty of their doctors and doctors' sons, the very best men and boys of the tribe, were murdered for their ill-successes in treating this epidemic. It seems that in that section, they have not left a single doctor alive.[59]

Once a shaman was slain, he was cremated. Encircling Paiutes, armed with willow whips, were at the ready to deal with any evil spirits that might escape the burning body. Every so often, shouting and wildly flailing, they would drive them off into the night.

59 *Inyo Independent*, November 11, 1876, p. 3.

The local whites (who had brought this about) were horror-stricken. Here was proof: native Americans were savages. Self-righteously, the whites sought to stop the killings, to little or no avail.

For the Paiutes, it was a time of confusion and terror. Not only were they demonized, but they were scared to death of ghosts of murdered shamans wreaking havoc among the living. The ghosts could snatch a family member as company on their journey-of-no-return to the land of the dead. Or they could shape-change to coyotes and visit further, vengeful illness.

At the same time—from the 1870s on—an even greater crisis was at hand and escalating. For the Paiutes, for all the desert tribes. For the Kumeyaay, the Cahuilla, the Quechan, the Chemehuevi, the Mojaves, the Shoshone, and a host of smaller, fragile groups.

Shamans had forever saved the souls of individuals. That was their calling.

They would now be called upon to save the souls of their clans, their tribes, their culture.

The challenge was daunting, and near-impossible.

Twilight

As an aspect of their calling, shamans prophesized future events—often disasters, a flood, drought, famine, or epidemic.

Or, as a Paiute foretold, "a people from across the ocean would come to take the country." Every night he would recite a list of the mountains in his tribe's territory, and rue that if no action was taken, they would soon be overrun and lost.

Dwelling on this, a Cahuilla was astonishingly explicit.

> One old man saw in a dream that men with skins the color of the dead, carrying sticks that spit fire, and riding animals like deer pulling objects that had round things that went round and round [wagon wheels?] were coming.[60]

60 Reported by Victoria Wierick. In John Lowell Bean, *Mukat's People*, p. 113.

Shamans at the time paid little heed. Only later would they regret that they had not combined their powers to stop, or at least hinder, the encroachment of invading whites. One reason: as far back as the passage of the Anza expedition in 1775 AD, they were caught up in demonstrating and contesting their powers.

Who would triumph as a shaman of shamans?

Shaman Contests

There would be public performances—contests—witnessed by dozens, even hundreds of tribesmen. Gathered in villages, they'd watch as shamans theatrically sought to outdo each other.

A shaman would spy a dove, clap his hands, and the dove would fall dead, blood flowing from its mouth. He would then pick the bird up, throw it in the air, and it would fly off. Another shaman would wash his

Shamans in supernatural combat. Little Petroglyph Canyon, western Mojave Desert.

hair with hot coals; then a rival would do him one better, and devour the coals. Yet another would pull his entrails out through his mouth, then stuff them back inside. Or so it appeared.

Often, there would be "shoot outs," duels in which shamans would attempt to "kill" each other by hurling poisonous invisible objects—magical airshots. A victim would clutch his chest, vomit blood, and collapse. Bystanders would be stunned. But then the hurler would stride to the man, doctor him, blow on him, and he would arise to dance before a relieved crowd. What better demonstration of a shaman's power than bringing a fellow shaman back to life? Raising him from the dead.

A shaman would be praised for his power, or if found lacking, would be ridiculed and dismissed.

The contests escalated. Shamans from one tribe would challenge those of another. There's an account of a contingent of a Las Vegas band of Paiutes journeying west to vie with the Cahuilla. These Las Vegas shamans were a showy lot; indeed, their excesses and parading of power were frowned upon by fellow Paiutes. In the case of Runs-Like-a-Mockingbird:

> While the man sang he would pick up some sort of plant, and as he held it in his hand, it flowered and bore fruit. He was able, too, to restore life to dead animals—quail, desert tortoise, and rabbits. But all this was not curing. A doctor who did such things never lasted long; he overdid.[61]

When the Las Vegas shamans arrived at a Cahuilla gathering,

> Everyone was waiting. After sundown a fire was built and each doctor showed his powers. Some made smoke come out of their

61 This and the following quote from Isabel T. Kelly, "Southern Paiute Shamanism," p. 163 & 164.

The shamans' split mountain, western Sonoran Desert.

> toes. Others brought black stink bugs out of their ears. Toward morning, a [Las Vegas] boy said, "Make a hot fire; use mesquite wood." He walked in the midst of the fire and sat down. All the spectators could see him melting away. They could hear the fire sizzling. The Cahuilla said, "We have lost a man!" Then at sunrise, when there were only ashes left, they saw him walking toward them smiling. The Cahuilla said, "You have beaten us; we cannot do that."

So it was that many shamans, caught up in magic for magic's sake, were not only remiss in their curing duties, but had little heed for rumor and the reality of the advance of the white man. Instead shaman contests—real or imagined—took on titanic proportions, with in one case, Cahuilla doctors facing off high on a mountain: "The doctors were so powerful in the old days that they split the mountain down one side and, and white sand comes down that side now."[63]

62 Florence C. Shipek, *Delfina Cuero, Her Autobiography*, p. 50.

Coincidentally, in December of 1775, led by Capt. Juan Bautista de Anza, Alta California's first settlers were to camp in the shadow of this very mountain on their way north to San Francisco. And what next transpired can be seen as the story of *the horse, the cross, and the steamboat.*

The Horse

A few weeks earlier, as the de Anza expedition crossed the Colorado River, the local Quechan had been so awed by the expedition's horses that they offered them acorns and valuable shells, the same gifts given the Spaniards. And from that day on, the exploration—and exploitation—of Alta California's deserts can be tracked by images of horses in rock art.

A shaman's cave, northern Mojave Desert.
To the far right, a horse and rider (enlarged in inset).
The Old Spanish Trail ran thirty miles south.

Dozens of such images survive—of an animal three times the size of a bighorn sheep and charged with extraordinary power, for they were joined to "men with skins the color of the dead, carrying sticks that spit fire." On one level, a shaman was recording a puzzling creature; on another, he may have hoped to gain its power. This was to give rise a new specialty: horse shamans—with dream horses their spirit helpers. They would sing to and soothe tribesman kicked, stomped, or thrown from the animal. Or they would minister to wounded horses—as, in effect, shaman-veterinarians.

The Cross

A prehistoric Kumeyaay cross.

Unlike the horse, the Spaniard's holy cross would not have puzzled or dumbfounded desert shamans.

They had crosses of their own, either as symbols of the morning or evening star, or to mark the four cardinal directions. Shamans were nevertheless intrigued by the Catholic cross, enough to depict it in their rock art. Just why, one wonders? The probable answer: to co-opt something—anything—with demonstrable power to serve their magical ends.

At the same time, this symbol and its power—which shamans may have believed they were co-opting—had native Americans flocking to be baptized into what the men in the brown robes proclaimed to be the only true religion. Catholicism, initially at least, had its appeal. As in legend the desert tribes had either killed their maker (the Cahuilla) or sequestered him in a remote Dark House (the Quechan), Spanish priests offered an intact, all-powerful creator-god. A god with more power than the sum of the land's shamans. Through the intercession of saints (not shamans), he was accessible to the littlest child and the oldest man or woman. Any and all who venerated the Christian cross and lived a Christian life would be granted a glorious eternal life.

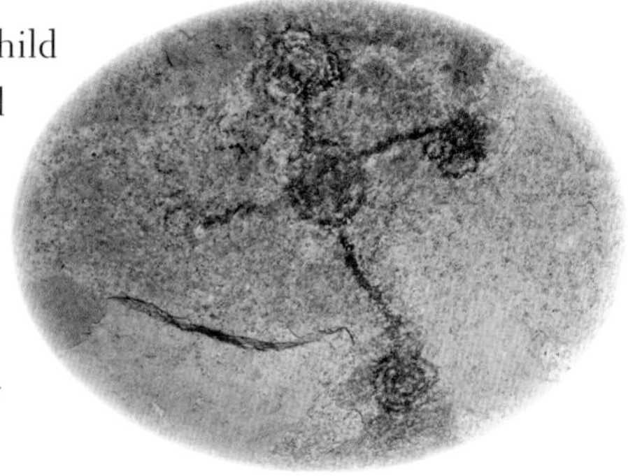

A budded mission-style, Catholic cross.

Lest there be any hesitation or reluctance accepting this, there was the ready threat of eternal damnation in a fiery, devil-stoked netherworld.

Given this, it is amazing that native Americans were to resist this combined promise and threat. Yet they did, particularly in desert hinterlands where the wonder of animals, clouds, the sun, the moon, and all nature held sway, and the hymns and harangues of the Catholic clergy were but the murmur of a distant wind.

Out there, in the desert's country of lost borders, shamanism would persist—and for a time, thrive.

The Steamboat

In the heart of the Mojave Desert, Corn Springs was a crossroads oasis, visited by the Cahuilla, the Quechan, and traders from numerous other tribes. Among the site's many petroglyphs there is one that would appear to be a canoe on wheels, and that indeed may have been the description relayed to the man who pecked it.

The year was likely 1858, with a messenger breathlessly reporting a little, smoke-belching paddlewheel steamboat venturing up the Colorado River.

By now, the desert's Indians had spied teams of horses and creaking wagons; they'd encountered gun-bearing soldiers and cross-waving missionaries. But they had confronted nothing quite like this. As reported

Corn Springs, southern Mojave Desert.

On the Colorado River, sixty miles east of Corn Springs: the Explorer, steamboat of the Ives Expedition.

by the expedition's leader, Joseph Christmas Ives, the local Chemehuevi reacted with an "expression of bewilderment and awe. The stern wheel particularly excites remarks. It is painted red, their favorite color, and why it should turn around without anyone touching it is the theme of constant wonder."[63] As well, onlookers were bemused by the *Explorer's* "slow progress a source of intense satisfaction and fun to the spectators on the banks. . . . Every time she ran aground a peal of laughter would ring from the bank."

Not long and hilarity was to give way to grief, in that the expedition's "Dr. Newberry found indications of gold, silver, lead, iron, and copper, and discovered veins resembling the gold-bearing rocks of California. A careful search might develop ample stores of treasure." The commentary did not bode well. Soon, larger steamboats plied the river, to disgorge not only people, but puzzling, ominous devices and supplies. Boilers, steam-driven engines, reels of cable, giant rock-crushing hammers—mining machinery to sate the white man's craving for precious metals. To fuel this, the desert's few and fragile forests would be cut down, and its springs tapped and emptied by miles of iron pipe.

To feed miners, ranches were established. Towns were then platted; rails were laid. The desert's Indians were restricted to reservations, bleak fragments of their once-grand lands. Little wonder that, disposed and demoralized, many turned to alcohol, and fell to indolence punctuated by bouts of violence.

Wovoka and the Ghost Dance

But hope was not lost, not yet. In 1889, a shaman of the Paiute Walker River Reservation inspired a renewal of Indian identity.

63 This and the following quotes from Joseph C. Ives, *Report upon the Colorado River of the West,* p. 59, 66, 56–57.

Jack Wilson, better known as Wovoka.

Wovoka, it was said, could conjure icicles in the palm of his hand, and at his command on a summer day a block of ice fell from the sky—feats of a weather shaman. He would invite a dead-on shotgun blast, and be none the worse for it. On New Year's Day of 1889, a solar eclipse darkened the Nevada sky, and lent him a vision—a "Great Revelation"—that old Paiute ways would return, and forever be honored. As described by James Mooney, an "Indian man" (U.S. government ethnographer) of Wovoka's acquaintance:

> On this occasion "the sun died" and he fell asleep in the daytime and was taken up to the other world. Here he saw God, with all the people who had died long ago engaged in their old time sport and occupations, all happy and forever young. It was a pleasant land and full of game. After showing him all, God told him he must go back and tell his people they must be good and love one another, have no quarreling, and live in peace with the whites. . . . If they faithfully obeyed his instructions they would at last be reunited with their friends in this other world. He was given the dance which he was commanded to bring back to his people. By performing this dance at intervals, for five consecutive days each time, they would secure this happiness to themselves and hasten the event.[64]

Belief in Wovaka's vision spread south through the desert to the lands of the Chemehuevi, but apparently not to the Kumeyaay, Cahuilla, and Quechan. Rather, it swept eastward like a prairie fire to the Indians of the Plains. It was there—at Wounded Knee—that alarmed whites instigated a massacre of Lakotas traveling to a Ghost Dance. Wovoka's overzealous followers had let it be known that the new religion prophesied that whites in the West would be beset by catastrophes; the earth would open up and swallow them. Regretably, Wovoka did little in the way of denying this.

A decade, and the time of the Ghost Dance was over.

It didn't help that Wavoka appears to have acknowledged Jesus Christ as "a pale Messiah," and was thereupon baptized. Even so, he still was a shaman, though dispensing with traditional lengthy rituals; "Not all night long! Didn't have to!" When Wovoka himself fell ill, he sought treatment not at the hands of fellow shamans, but in the offices of Anglo doctors.

64 James Mooney, "The Ghost Dance Religion and the Sioux Outbreak of 1890," p. 771–2.

Ghost Dancers of the Plains.
Photographs by James Mooney, an acquaintance of Wovoka.

Even to those who knew him well, Wovoka's personality was elusive. He was said to be smart, sly, good-hearted, a rogue, and "if anybody ever got the Indian's beliefs of Medicine jumbled up with the white man's belief in Christianity, and mixed them into a fine, confusing brew, it was Wovoka."[65]

A Methodist preacher laid Jack Wilson—Wovoka—to rest.

Into the Twentieth Century

For Pauites at the turn of the twentieth century, the shaman had, at best, a secondary role in doctoring, and as "a man of power." He operated in the shadow of the lawman, often an Indian lawman.

Yet for all the battering inflicted by priest, miners, settlers, and the U.S. government, shamanism in the desert was to survive well into the twentieth century.

With holdouts ranging from caves of the Coso Mountains to peaks of Baja California—and, unexpectedly, the environs of Palm Springs, even as its settlement became a destination for sun-seeking tourists.

To this day, a principal Palm Springs street is Vista Chino—in honor of shaman Pedro Chino.

Twentieth century Cahuilla shaman Pedro Chino, it was held, could sense trouble far distant. He then would shape-shift to a swift animal, or plunge into a spring, and fly through underground channels to wherever a soul was in need. With a skyward wave of his hand (to the usual realm of magical flight), he'd say, "To me it is just like this underground." In the blink of an eye he could whisk from Palm Springs on one side if the San Jacinto Mountains to Soboba Springs on the other, and do this—with hardly a heed for malign water babies.

65 Wovoka friend Tim McCoy, a silent movie star, in *Tim McCoy Remembers the West*, p. 221.

Above: Forlorn Paiute shaman Oich Johnson.
Right: A fellow Paiute vested in a suit, watch, and badge—regalia of a white lawman.

Scattered allusions to water babies appear in shamans' accounts throughout the desert. A bubbling spring meant that they were down there, breathing; and hot springs, it was held, were created by their cooking fires. It was at the springs of Palm Springs that they were given a final mention, and their role clarified. Pedro Chino described one haunting its waters: "It lives down there. You can hear him cry at night. It sounds like a little baby crying. Nobody sees it. If you see it . . . something is going to happen to your family."[66]

Water babies were believed to have created rock art—and then guarded it with a curse upon any who approached and touched it.

Palm Springs chief Francisco Patencio told the tale a water baby with "pure white skins and hair." Children fetching water thought it to be more animal than human.

> One girl picked it up in her arms. Then a whirlwind came, and lifted the two in the air, then settled over the water, and both the girl and the child disappeared down the spring.
>
> The next morning the body of the girl came up, but she was dead.[67]

Alas now, sadly, a chronicle of the lives of desert shamans would share the fate of that little girl.

The Last of the Desert Shamans

As Francisco Patencio was the Cahuilla's last great chief, Pedro Chino was the tribe's last "shaman of shamans." They served their tribe into the 1920s, while at the same time, north across the desert, Bob Rabbit, the last known Shoshone/Kawaii rain shaman, was believed

66 Quoted in Deborah Dozier, *The Heart Is Fire*, p. 56.
67 Chief Francisco Patencio, *Stories and Legends of the Palm Springs Indian*, p. 92.

Above: Cahuilla shaman Pedro Chino home for dinner and, if summoned, a night of doctoring. *Left:* Pedro Chino was not only a pul—a shaman—but a pa'v'ul—a powerful shaman of shamans.

to have executed a farewell panel of pictographs under the overhang of a massive boulder.

Subsequently, in northern Baja California in the late 1930s, a last, heated contest between Kumeyaay shamans was reportedly held high on the flank of their sacred Mount Cu'ma' (Tecate Mountain).

And in the 1940s and beyond, neighboring Cahuillas initiated a concerted effort to preserve their knowledge and practice of age-old botanical cures, but at the same time witnessed their shamans, one by one, ageing and dying—and with them, their craft, lore, and magic.

A calling that had spiritually sustained a thousand and more desert generations was fast fading.

In his last days, an elderly Cahuilla was to sadly shake his head:

With a stone tube, Cahuilla Francesco Lugo listens to spirit voices.

> There was a lot of Indian people here at one time. There is no more. There is no longer any dances, ceremonial dances. There is no eagle dance. Nothing is there anymore.
>
> The kids, the children that are left now, will never know what it was.
>
> This is the way it will be, this is the way it is. It is finished. It is done. It is understood. We do not know what it will be now. Everything is disappearing. I am the one that is talking now, Perfecto Segundo. I am 74 years old.[68]

This Perfecto Segundo was a venerated shaman.

68 Quoted in Deborah Dozier, *The Heart Is Fire*, p. 141.

Right: Panel attributed to Bob Rabbit.
Below: To the left, Bob Rabbit's boulder.
Coso Mountains, western Mojave Desert.

And Now . . .

Despite the shaman Segundo's epitaph, a lingering question remains: Might shamans still work their magic? Though there is no clear evidence for this, there are hints. Preston Arrow-weed, a Quechan acquaintance of the author, recalls the blind shaman White Mud and his ability to heal a broken neck; as well, he recalls a childhood confrontation with a shaman "with the power to kill just by looking at you." (He was dissuaded from harming young Preston by Preston's uncle, Red Bean.) As to present times, Arrow-weed admits, "Shamans . . . they're around," but is uncomfortable offering further details. A cross-section of members of additional tribes had similar responses. A Kumeyaay, whose father was a shaman, allowed, "In the last century, it [shamanism] went underground. It still goes on . . . a fair amount." He then added, "We're a particularly stubborn group. We like to keep things close to the vest. We don't share such things."

Michael Madrigal is a Cahuilla known for his spirituality, and his work to reconcile, when possible, native American and European traditions. He is at once a Catholic lay minister and a Bird Singer versed in the saga of his tribe's ancient wanderings. He offers a perspective that was at once carefully thought-out and emotionally compelling.

> So many of the old ways were lost that here in Soboba [his reservation] and then over in Morongo, with the result that Big Houses of both [ceremonial centers] were burned and put to sleep. And with them went the role, the power of shamans. Even so, what shamans were aware of and experienced, remains—in songs, stories, sacred sites, plants, and animals. All of these, we believe, are blessed with *iva'a*—living spirits. Even rocks have iva'a. Rocks are ancient ones, our oldest teachers.

> All nature, you see, is populated by spirits, alive in our community's heart.
>
> And dreams, they too are important. As in the past, they deliver messages. They warn. They teach.

He spoke of a recent encounter with ancient belief. "A relative had died, but was not at peace." There were disturbances, in the course of which, "Someone saw his spirit, and was afraid it would frighten the children." Michael was asked for his help. Though a devout Christian, he burned sage; he purified the air with an eagle feather. He prayed. And the spirit fled.

> Yes, the shamans may be gone. But we, the Cahuilla, are still here; and iva'a is still here—in the spirit of us as a people, in the spirit of our ancestors, in the spirit of the earth and all that's in it.

He nodded, then smiled as he reflected:

> You know, from my childhood, I remember my mother and aunt telling about a shaman making a beaver pelt wriggle and move all by itself. They said it was strange, even scary. As well, there was talk of Ambrosio the fire-eater. And we all heard stories of shamans who could dive into the hot springs here in Soboba and in no time rise from the springs over in Palm Springs.

And one may wonder: Was there a time—and a way beyond our comprehension—when they could do such things?

Epilogue

The pursuit of *Old Magic* led Bonnie and me down many a desert road. On a paved highway, we'd be advised, "Next Gas 74 Miles," and there would be not even a shack in the interval. There would be sandy tracks of uncertain inclination. "I think they want us to go over there, sort of to that butte." Along the way, there was ever time for rumination. In describing trances, had we sought logic where chaos reigned? Had we gone too far in hazarding interpretations of rock art?

Low desert or high, the landscape often had us wondering what it may have been like in the time of the shamans. What trails ran where? Up there, just below the ridge, was there a hidden dream quest site? We would discuss the uncertain, elusive nature of shamans. Some, no doubt, were sorcerers. And many were scoundrels. But most sought order in the stars and in the mysteries and wonder of their grand, if unforgiving landscape. When summoned, they doctored the stricken, be they stoic elders or frightened little children. They conjured rains. Taking leave of

A tiny shaman's hearth. Like a whirlwind, it could transport a shaman to a supernatural world.

reality, they rode whirlwinds and soared in magical flight. They epitomized a native American ability "to relate to the land in ways beyond a Western way of thinking."[70]

With arcane knowledge gained in the shining darkness of their dream quests, these numerous men and few women were adept in the practice of old magic. That old magic may be no more or still exist underground. Either way, it is hardly forgotten—with credit due early twentieth-century ethnographers, and

69 Conversation with Mountain Cahuilla Michael Madrigal, October, 2009.

A whirlwind spiral and a shaman. Little Petroglyph Canyon, Western Mojave Desert.

their shaman informants who generously and patiently recounted their cures and adventures.

A summer ago, south of the settlement of Shoshone on California 95, fingers of grit and dust rose from the earth. A whirlwind formed and hovered by the highway. We slowed and stopped.

"Ever been hit by one? I haven't."

"Oh yes," Bonnie replied, "It was scary. Sand, gravel, branches, entire shrubs spinning around. . . . And I wonder, I really wonder, what Indians back then would have thought of whirlwinds," she thought out loud, "Fury in the still air."

"A shaman on his way. . . ."

Not long, and there were six to eight whirlwinds in sight.

A few wound down and died away.

Two were last seen crossing the Funeral Range in the direction of Death Valley—to the "sacred land, mythic country" of the northern desert tribes. A land steeped in old magic.

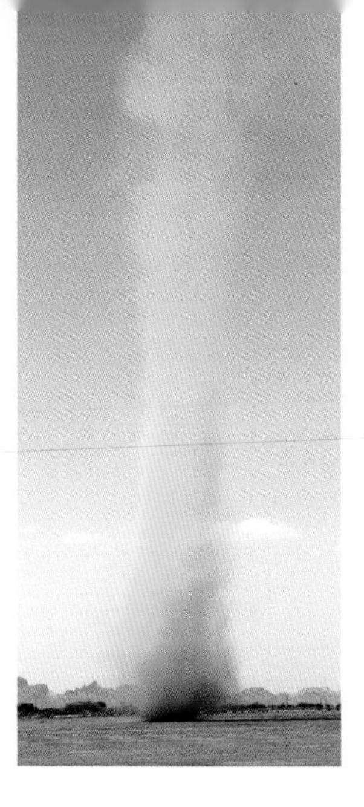

Notes and Acknowledgments

Part One:
THE WAY OF THE SHAMAN

Dawn

The author's awareness of the life and lore of American Indians harkens to his eighth year. A family friend, Watson Smith, represented Harvard's Peabody Museum of Anthropology in matters west of the Pecos River, and visiting us, he wove tales of living with the Zuni and excavating ancient Awatovi, where he found a way to preserve multiple layers of kiva murals—a critical step in the understanding of Indian imagery.

Living in the desert town of Borrego Springs, my wife, Bonnie, and I have attended ceremonies and met with Indians at several nearby reservations, and we particularly thank Michael Madrigal of the Mountain Cahuilla and Preston Arrow-weed of the Quechan for time spent with us. We are as well indebted to William Contreras of the Desert Cahuilla for an initial account of his tribe's creation. Not wanting to pry, I was hesitant to ask about this. He in turn told the tale of Mukat and his people at the core of this chapter. This would be the first of many, many questions as to the world of the desert shaman. Fortunately, quite a number were answered in interviews conducted by Alfred Kroeber's fledgling Berkeley anthropologists—who found shamans of the desert quite open in describing their calling and cures.

The idea that in legend the Cahuilla had willfully killed Mukat, their creator, is, to say the least, unsettling. But it also appears that the Cahuilla have since come to honor *Umna'ah* (literally: "the Huge One")—a version of the "Great Spirit" at the core of the belief systems of nearly all American tribes. I thank Tom Fredericks, of Lakota descent, for explaining that this "Great Spirit" is as well the "Great Mystery" in that it eludes explanation and understanding. But, as Tom pointed out, this is not necessary. "What is important is that it exists, it simply is." As an analogy, Tom described the reflection of the moon in a pool of water. "You see it. It's there. But you can't grasp it."

Suffice it to say that in spirit the Cahuilla were at one with the spirit of all nature, all creation.

Signs

This chapter would not have been possible without Ruby Modesto's *Not for Innocent Ears*. A Cahuilla medicine woman immersed in shamanism, she is forthright—irrepressible, actually—in her vivid memories and descriptions.

Coming of Age

Here and throughout the book, I've relied on multiple sources (credited in the Selected Bibliography), and seeking to fit them together—a fact here, a description there—was akin to working a jigsaw puzzle. Initially mystifying, at the end a rounded picture.

I often consulted (and would recommend as further reading):

1925	A.L. Kroeber, *Handbook of the Indians of California.* A classic compendium, as relevant today as when it was written.
1931	C. Daryll Forde, *Ethnography of the Yuma Indians.* Beliefs and rite along the Colorado River.
1938	Willard Z. Park, *Shamanism in Western North America.* A focused study based on interviews with several shamans.
1951	Mircea Eliade, *Shamanism: Archaic Techniques of Ecstasy.* A world survey.
1972	Lowell John Bean, *Mukat's People.* An in-depth account of the life of the Cahuilla.
1980	Ruby Modesto and Guy Mount, *Not For Innocent Ears.* Previously cited.
1984–2005	Ken Hedges, *Rock Art Papers.* New frontiers in the recording, conservation, and interpretation of the West's petroglyphs and pictographs.
1992	Lowell John Bean, ed., *California Indian Shamanism.* A selection of diverse, informative papers.
2002	James L. Pearson, *Shamanism and the Ancient Mind.* Explores the question: Can archaeology shed light on human cognition?

In this chapter I debated how to portray a shaman's demonstration of his magic—which clearly involved sleight of hand and like hocus-pocus. But then: In our day and age, do we attend a theatrical performance and carp about its artifice? On the contrary, in a willing suspension of disbelief, we enjoy, even revel in its stagecraft. And every so often, we pronounce the experience life-changing. Why not the same regard for the desert's old magic?

In April of 2008, Bonnie discovered the badlands star chart site explored in this chapter. As I was busily documenting a series of prehistoric cairns, she called down from the edge of a nearby mesa, "Nick, there's something up here you just might want to have a look at." There certainly was, but we would never have made sense of it had it not been for related sand paintings decoded a hundred years ago—at the behest of anthropologist T.T. Waterman—by Kumeyaay elders Manual Lachusa, Antonio Maces, and Jo Waters.

California State Park archaeologist Joan Schneider was to note (which I had not) that the desert floor within the circle had been trampled and compacted, evidence of its long-term ritual use.

And I thank archaeo-astronomer Dr. E.C. Krupp for not only reviewing our findings (and offering corrections), but publishing them in the journal *Griffith Observer.*

At the Edge of the Village

Outstanding examples of magic mountains are to be found at Corn Springs in the southern Mojave, at the western Nevada sites of Grapevine Canyon and Atlatl Rock.

Paraphernalia & Regalia

Serendipity offered a photograph of Shoshone Bill Kawitch in the archive of Tonopah's Central Nevada Museum, and then a companion picture posing with his wife in the collection of Reno's Nevada Historical Society.

Little Petroglyph Canyon in California's Coso Mountains is an unrivaled grand gallery of shaman-self depiction and related imagery. Though on a military base, it can be accessed by well-run tours offered by the nearby Maturango Museum. The museum's Eva Younkin has edited an informative volume, *Coso Rock Art: A New Perspective*, and David Whitley has provided a step-by-step guide to the site, *Following the Shaman's Path.*

Doctoring

The circumstances and ceremony related in this chapter are basically Cahuilla. However, since curing was remarkably the same throughout the deserts of the far West, quotes have been added from shamans of other tribes, notably Manual Thomas of the Quechan and Joe Green of the northern Paiutes.

For curing, there were some odd—though logical—choices of spirit helpers. A mouse or packrat "could steal the disease away." A bat's alleged ability to freeze water could cure burns or reduce fevers.

Sorcerers

The concept that power was amoral was by no means unique to native Americans. In Judaism, Christianity, and Islam, angels wrestle with demons, with power accessible to both.

Further, the evil shamans Tahquitz and Tamiotemevie echo Christianity's Satan—looming, horrific, and a *numetuked*, "an eater of people" in the mythology of the Paiute.

Part Two: DREAM QUEST

Circles and Caves

Anza-Borrego Desert State Park Superintendent Mark Jorgensen was ever encouraging and helpful as Bonnie and I pursued this project. And staff archaeologists Joan Schneider and Sue Wade have our appreciation for interpreting and protecting the park's Indian heritage.

I thank Death Valley rambler and historian Chuck Knight for a hike to a cave little changed since its last shaman awoke from a dream quest and walked away, never to return.

A note on the chemistry of toloache (a datura extract): Targeting the central nervous system and rife with alkaloids, datura is a powerful, disassociative hallucinogen. The depressant scopolamine initiates drowsiness and sleep, and can erase prior-life memory; atropine disables muscles and dilates eyes. The combination conjures vivid dreams that at once are wildly surreal and realistically convincing.

Trances: Taking Leave / Transformation / With the Spirits

The arc of these three chapters seeks to capture the wild, other-worldly nature of a shaman's dream quest. For what they psychically dared and ventured, they deserve credit and even admiration. In the course of an interview with present-day Quechan Preston Arrow-weed, he was to chuckle, then comment, "You know, we laugh in the face of death. Back then—and today. Today as well."

I thank Donald Austin, proprietor of http://petroglyphs.us , for helping me survey little-known shamanic images. His CDs of rock art sites are guides to their range and themes.

For a perspective on the interpretation of rock in recent decades, I in debt to Ken Hedges and his *Rock Art Papers*, published annually by San Diego's Museum of Man.

Journey to the Land of Fire

I long had an image of Indian tribes occupying a fixed territory and generally keeping to themselves. I was surprised to learn how frequently and far individuals traveled—to trade, acquire knowledge, and see for themselves a world beyond their village.

If there is an epicenter of the deserts of the far West, it is Death Valley. Westerners have called it everything from a "a pit of horrors" to "a palace of dreams, . . . a place of strange, terrible happiness." And long before these words were penned, it was the Indian's *Tomesha*, awesome and sacred, as were the nearby Coso Mountains, a haunt of weather shamans.

It is probable that shamans controlling the weather had a workable knowledge of the signs and patterns of desert weather—the times of day winds would rise or die away, the look of clouds promising rain, the likely duration of a storm.

Pursuit of a Lost Soul

This chapter considers a complex of petroglyphs high on the Valley of Fire's Atlatl Rock (see pp.154–156). Several interpretations are possible. It has been suggested that here is a map of a happy hunting ground, thus the atlatl—a primitive throwing stick—at the top of the panel. Or the panel could illustrate a tale of twins as links, in Indian mythology, between the quick and the dead. I thought an account of a dream quest to the land of the dead to be the most likely, but I could be wrong. Or finally, how about this: the panel could embody *all three* interpretations.

In the Owens Valley town of Independence, I thank the Inyo County Free Library, and curator Beth Porter at the Eastern Californian Museum for ferreting out newspaper reports and a rare image bearing on an 1876 mass killing of shamans.

There were further kill-offs. In 1877, a smallpox epidemic decimated the Quechan. This "proved particularly disastrous to the medicine men, and the office frequently went begging for occupants." (E.J. Trippel, "The Yuma Indians," p. 570)

A decade later the sad story was repeated in a kill-off of shamans on the Paiute Walker River reservation.

Twilight

I wish I didn't have to write this chapter, the story of a long tradition of healing magic fading away, fated to become old magic. As his friend Andy Vitovitch said of the originator of the Ghost Dance, "Poor old Wovoka. They run him down."

The Making of *Old Magic*

Old Magic's search for historic shaman-related images was aided by the generous help and advice of Alan Jutzi of the Huntington Library; Beth

Davenport of the archives of Death Valley National Park; Eva LaRue and Angela Haig of the Central Nevada Museum; Lee Brumbaugh of the Nevada Historical Society, and Guy Mount, co-author of Ruby Modesto's reminiscences of her life as a shaman.

For extraordinary present-day images, I'm indebted to photographer and image processing whiz David Meltzer. And to Manfred Knaak, Dennis Mammana, Joan Rosen, Jim Wark, and Kevin Price.

An early draft was considerably improved by extensive notes and advice offered by Martha Joukowsky, President-emeritus of the Archaeological Institute of America.

And I can't say enough about the enthusiastic staff at Sunbelt Publications. Editors Diana and Lowell Lindsay helped shape a point-of-view exploring the world of desert shamans. At their behest, rock art expert Steve Freers reviewed *Old Magic*'s manuscript and offered a perspective as to how to both describe and protect sensitive sites. As well, there couldn't be a better (and calmer) Publication Manager than Debi Young, and designer Lydia D'moch imaginatively created an interplay between text and images.

In Memoriam

Armand Frederick Vallée

1921 – 2009

In the course of a long and distinguished career, internationally acclaimed artist Armand Vallée roamed the deserts of the Far West. He sought to capture their wonder and magic—in visions that reflected an awe of nature shared by his Kumeyaay and Cahuilla acquaintances. He affirmed, "Nature has nourished and sustained my spiritual well-being."

In his work, Vallée often found himself in a dream state. He wrote, "When I paint, it is like walking in a dream and entering into an endless universe." It was only natural, then, that he touch on the calling and life of a desert shaman.

Armand Vallée gifted many of his paintings to his friends at the Native American Land Conservancy.

TIME SPIRIT
Rising above the badlands of Anza-Borrego Desert State Park,
a circular, swirling sky challenges a shaman to pursue a dream quest.
Where this will lead is enigmatic, even ominous.

ONCE UPON A TIME
In a shaman's psychic journeys, spirit helpers were his guides,
teachers - and second self.

Selected Bibliography

Barrows, David P., *The Ethnobotany of the Coahuilla Indians of Southern California* (Chicago: University of Chicago Press, 1900)

Bean, Lowell John, "California Indian Shamanism and Folk Curing," in Lowell J. Bean, ed., *California Indian Shamanism* (Menlo Park, CA; Ballena Press, 1992)

___, "Power and Its Applications in Native California," in Bean, *California Indian Shamanism*

___, *Mukat's People: The Cahuilla Indians of Southern California* (Berkeley: University of California Press, 1972)

___, "The Shamanic Experience," in Bean, *California Indian Shamanism.*

Bean, Lowell J. and Katherine Siva Saubel, *Temalpakh: Cahuilla Indian Knowledge of Usage of Plants* (Morongo Indian Reservation: Malki Museum Press, 1972)

Bean, Lowell J. and Sylvia B. Vance, "California Religious Systems and Their Transformations," in Bean, *California Indian Shamanism*

Bock, Frank, "The Great Galleries of the Coso Range: California's Most Extensive Rock Art Site" in J. Van Tilburg, ed., *Ancient Images on Stone* (Los Angeles: UCLA Rock Art Archive, 1983)

Campbell, Paul D., *Earthen Pigments and Paint of the California Indians* (Los Angeles: Paul Douglas Campbell, 2007)

Castaneda, Carlos, *The Teachings of Don Juan: A Yaqui Way of Knowledge* (Berkeley: University of California Press, 1969)

Chalfant, W.A., *The Story of Inyo* (Bishop, CA: Chalfant Press, 1933)

Dozier, Deborah, *The Heart Is Fire: The World of the Cahuilla Indians of Southern California* (Berkeley: Heydey Books, 1998)

DuBois, Constance G., "The Mythology of the Diegueños, *Journal of American Folk-Lore*, vol. 14, no. 54 (1901)

Eliade, Mircea, *Shamanism: Archaic Techniques of Ecstasy* (Princeton: Princeton University Press, 1964)

Font, Father Pedro, "The Colorado Yumans in 1775" in R.F. Heizer and M.A. Whipple, *The California Indians: a Source Book* (Berkeley: University of California Press, 1971)

Forde, C. Daryll, *Ethnography of the Yuma Indians* (Berkeley: University of California Press, 1931)

Furst, Peter T. and Richard E. Schultes, *Flesh of the Gods* (New York: Praeger Publishing, 1972)

Grant, Campbell, James W. Baird and J. Kenneth Pringle, *Rock Drawings of the Coso Range* (Ridgecrest, CA: Maturango Museum, 1987)

Harrington, John P., "The Chemehuevi: Their Name, Character, and Habitat" in *Harrington Papers*, reels 89–93 (Washington, D.C.: National Anthropological Archives, Smithsonian Institution: Northern and Central California, n.d.)

Hedges, Ken, "Southern California Rock Art as Shamanistic Rock Art" in *American Indian Rock Art* 2, American Rock Art Research Association, 1976

___, "Rock Art Records of Belief and Knowledge" in *Archaeology of San Diego and Southern California* (San Diego: Archaeological Institute of America, 1981)

___, "Phosphenes in the Context of Native American Rock Art" in American Indian Rock Art 7–8, American Rock Art Research Association, 1982

___, "The Shamanistic Origins of Rock Art" in J. Van Tilburg, ed., *Ancient Images on Stone* (Los Angeles: UCLA Rock Art Archive, 1983)

___, ed., *Rock Art Papers*, vol. 1–17 (San Diego: San Diego Museum of Man, 1984–2005)

___, "Shamanistic Aspects of California Rock Art," in Bean, *California Indian Shamanism*

Hittman, Michael, *Wovoka and the Ghost Dance* (Lincoln, NB: University of Nebraska, 1997)

Hooper, Lucile, "The Cahuilla Indians" in *University of California Publications in American Archaeology and Ethnology*, vol. 16, no. 6 (April, 1920)

James, George Wharton, "The Legend of Tauquitch and Algoot" in Journal of American Folk-Lore, vol. 16, no. 62 (1093)

Johnson, Edward C., *Walker River Paiutes: a Tribal History* (Shurz, NV: Walker River Paiute Tribe, 1975)

Jones, Bernard M., Jr., "Sacred Paths, Mystical Dwellings and Cardinal Directions: Continuing Studies of Mountain Lion Symbolism," in Ken Hedges, ed., *Rock Art Papers*, vol. 15, San Diego Museum of Man, 2000

Halifax, Joan, *Shaman: the Wounded Healer* (London: Thames & Hudson, 1982)

___, "Shamanistic Symbols: Visual Metaphors in Rock Art Images," in Ken Hedges, ed., *Rock Art Papers*, vol. 16, San Diego Museum of Man, 2003

___, "Reflected Images of Power: Shamanistic Metaphors in Rock Art," in Ken Hedges, ed., *Rock Art Papers*, vol. 17, San Diego Museum of Man, 2005

Kaldenberg, Russell L., A *Festschrift Honoring the Contributions of California Archaeologist Jay von Werlhof* (Ridgecrest, CA: Maturango Museum, 2006)

Kaweit, Holger, *Shamans, Healers, and Medicine Men* (Boston: Shambala, 2000)

Kelly, Isabel T., "Chemehuevi Shamanism" in *Essays on Anthropology* (Berkeley: University of California, 1936)

___, "Southern Paiute Shamanism" in *University of California Anthropological Records*, vol. 2, no. 4 (Berkeley: University of California Press, 1939)

Klüver, Heinrich, *Mescal and Mechanisms of Hallucination* (Chicago: University of Chicago Press, 1966)

Knaak, Manfred, *The Forgotten Artist: Indians of Anza-Borrego and Their Rock Art* (Borrego Springs, CA: Anza-Borrego Desert Natural History Association, 1988)

Kroeber, A.L., "Ethnography of the Cahuilla Indians" in *University of California Publications in American Archaeology and Ethnology*, vol. 8, no. 2 (June, 1908)

___, *Handbook of the Indians of California* (New York: Dover, 1976), originally published in *Bulletin 78 of the Bureau of American Ethnology of the Smithsonian Institution* (Washington, D.C.: Government Printing Office, 1923)

Krupp, E.C., "Emblems in the Sky" in J. Van Tilburg, ed., *Ancient Images on Stone* (Los Angeles: UCLA Rock Art Archive, 1983)

Laird, Carobeth, *The Chemehuevis* (Banning, CA: Malki Museum Press, 1976)

___, *Mirror and Pattern* (Banning, CA: Malki Museum Press, 1984)

La Fave, Jeffrey F., "An Examination of Probably 'Cultural Contact' Rock Art Sites in Southern California and Northern Baja California," in Ken Hedges, ed., *Rock Art Papers*, vol. 17, San Diego Museum of Man, 2005

___, *A Cosmos in Stone: Interpreting Religion and Society Through Rock Art* (Walnut Creek, California: Altamira Press, 2002)

Lewis-Williams, J. David, *Cosmos in Stone* (Walnut Creek, California: AltaMira Press, 2002)

Mallery, Garrick, *Picture Writing of the American Indians* (Washington, D.C.: Government Printing Office, 1893)

McCoy, Tim, *Tim McCoy Remembers the West* (Lincoln, NB: University of Nebraska, 1977)

Miller, Jay, "Great Basin Religion and Theology: A Comparative Study of Power" in *Journal of California and Great Basin Anthropology*, vol. 5, no. 1, 1983

___, *Shamanistic Odyssey: the Lushootseed Salish Journey to the Land of the Death* (Menlo Park, CA: Ballena Press, 1988)

Modesto, Ruby and Guy Mount, *Not for Innocent Ears: Spiritual Traditions of a Desert Cahuilla Medicine Woman* (Cottonwood, CA: Sweetlight Books, 1980)

Mooney, James, "The Ghost Dance Religion and the Sioux Outbreak of 1890" in *Fourteenth Annual Report of the Bureau of Ethnology of The Smithsonian Institution, 1892–1893* (Washington, D.C.: Government Printing Office, 1896)

Nabakov, Peter, *Where Lightning Strikes: the Lives of American Indian Sacred Places* (New York: Viking Penguin, 2006)

Park, Willard Z., *Shamanism in Western North America* (Mansfield Centre, CT: Martino Publishing, 2007; originally published in Evanston & Chicago: Northwestern University Press, 1938)

Patencio, Chief Francisco, *Stories and Legends of the Palm Springs Indians* (Palm Springs, CA: Palm Springs Desert Museum, 1943

Paterson, Alex, A *Field Guide to Rock Art Symbols of the Greater Southwest* (Boulder, CO: Johnson Books, 1992)

Pearson, James L. *Shamanism and the Ancient Mind: a Cognitive Approach to Archaeology* (Walnut Creek, CA: AltaMira Pres, 2002)

Shipek, Florence C., *Delfina Cuero: Her Autobiography, an Account of*

Her Last Years, and Her Ethnobotanic Contributions (Menlo Park, CA: Ballena Press, 1991)

___, "The Shaman: Priest, Doctor, Scientist," in Bean, *California Indian Shamanism*

Smith, Gerald A., *The Mojaves* (San Bernadino, CA: San Bernadino County Museum, 1966)

___, "Geoglyphs, Rock Alignments, and Ground Figures" in J. Van Tilburg, ed., *Ancient Images on Stone* (Los Angeles: UCLA Rock Art Archive, 1983)

Smith, Gerald A. and Wilson G. Turner, *Indian Rock Art of Southern California* (San Bernadino, CA: San Bernadino County Museum, 1975)

Spier, Leslie, *Yuma Tribes of the Gila River* (New York: Cooper Square Publishers, 1970)

Strong, William D., *Aboriginal Society in Southern California* (Banning, CA: Malki Museum Press, Morongo Indian Reservation, 1978)

Trafzer, Clifford E., Luke Madrigal and Anthony Madigal, *Chemehuevi People of the Coachella Valley* (Coachella, CA: The Twenty-Nine Palms Band of Mission Indians, 1997)

Trippel, E.J., "The Yuma Indians" in *Overland Monthly*, 2nd series: 13 & 14, 1889

Von Werlhof, Jay, "Granite Galleries," in *Pacific Discovery*, vol. 11, no. 4, 1958

___, *Spirits of the Earth, vol. 1 & 2* (El Centro, CA: Imperial Valley College Museum, 1987 and 2004)

___, "E=MC2: Implications of Power in Yuha Desert Geoglyphs," in Ken Hedges, ed., *Rock Art Papers*, vol. 14, San Diego Museum of Man, 1999

Whitley, David S., A *Guide to Rock Art Sites: Southern California and Southern Nevada* (Missoula, MT: Mountain Press Publishing, 1996)

___, "Meaning and Metaphor in the Coso Petroglyphs" in Elva Younkin, ed., *Coso Rock Art* (Ridgecrest, CA: Maturango Museum, 1998)

___, *Following the Shaman's Path* (Ridgecrest, CA: Maturango Museum, 1998)

___, *The Art of the Shaman: Rock Art in California* (Salt Lake City, UT: University of Utah Press, 2000)

Whitley, David S., Tamara K. Whitley and Joseph M. Simon, *The Archaeology of Ayers Rock (CA-INY-134) California* (Ridgecrest, CA: Maturango Museum, 2005)

Younkin, Elva, ed., *Coso Rock Art: A New Perspective* (Ridgecrest, CA: Maturango Museum, 1998)

Photo Credits

Multiple photographs on a page are listed clockwise from upper left (a-b-c-d). Where known, photographers are credited in boldface.
Not listed: *color photographs taken by the author.*

Cover b	E.W. Smith/Central Nevada Historical Society
ii	Braun Research Library Collection, Autry National Center P.550
vi	**Kevin Price**
xv	Bancroft Library, University of California, Berkeley
xvii	**Manfred Knaak**/Anza-Borrego Desert Natural History Association
xviii	**Joan Rosen**
4–5	**Jim Wark**/AirPhoto
20	**Guy Mount**

22	**Edward S. Curtis**/Charles Deering Library of Special Collections,Northwestern University
23	**Steve Bier**
26	**Edward S. Curtis**/Charles Deering Library of Special Collections, Northwestern University
28	**Paul Douglas Campbell**
34	Hearst Museum of Anthropology
38	© **Dennis Mammana**/dennismammana.com
41	**Manfred Knaak**/Anza-Borrego Desert Natural History Association
53	**E.W. Smith**/Central Nevada Historical Society
56	**E.W. Smith**/Central Nevada Historical Society
57	**E.W. Smith**/Nevada Historical Society
58a	**David Meltzer**
58c	**David Meltzer**
60a	**David Meltzer**
61a	**David Meltzer**
62–63	**Edward S. Curtis**/Charles Deering Library of Special Collections, Northwestern University
70	San Diego Historical Society
71	Braun Research Library, Autry National Center P.2352
78a	**Manfred Knaak**/Anza-Borrego Desert Natural History Association
100–101a	**Donald Austin**/petroglyph.us
113c	**Jim & Jamie Dutcher**/National Geographic Creative
121	**Manfred Knaak,** Anza-Borrego Desert Natural History Association
132b	**Donald Austin**/petroglyph.us
138	**David Meltzer**
140b	**Paul Johnson**
142a–c	**David Meltzer**

145b	**David Meltzer**
146	**David Meltzer**
148	iStockphoto
149	**David Meltzer**
151	Nevada Historical Society
152a	iStockphoto
152b	**Donald Austin**/petroglyph.us
158–159	**Mary Austin**/Huntington Library
161	**James Mooney**/National Anthropological Archives
162	**David Meltzer**
168b	Huntington Library
170	Nevada Historical Society
172 a–b	**James Mooney**/National Anthropological Archives
174 a–b	Nevada Historical Society
176a–b	Palm Springs Historical Society
177	San Diego Historical Society
181	© **Dennis Mammana**/dennismammana.com
184	NASA
192–193	**Armand Vallée,** courtesy of Liesel Paris Art Studio & Gallery/valleeart.com
194	**David Meltzer**
201	**David Meltzer**
Back cover b	Bonnie Clapp

Index